MISSION POSSIBLE

Successful Women Entrepreneurs
Sharing Step-by-Step How to Become One

with

ALEASHA BAHR, CHRISTINA NICHOLSON, KARIANNE
MUNSTEDT, DORTHA HISE, KIVA SLADE, CAROLINA
M. BILLINGS, JENNY BELANGER, JEN HALL & ANNA
PASZKIET, STACY HERMAN LANG, GINA R. SMITH,
MELANIE HERSCHORN, HALLIE AGOSTINELLI

PWTPublishing
DIVERSITY INCLUSION EQUITY
A DIVISION OF POWERFUL WOMEN TODAY

Published by PWT Publishing

3 Centre St. #202,

Markham, ON L3P 3P9

Canada

Publisher Carolina M. Billings

Publisher Email: publisher@powerfulwomentoday.com

Limits of Liability and Disclaimer of Warranty

The author and publisher shall not be liable for the reader's misuse of this material. This book is for strictly informational and educational purposes.

Disclaimer

The views expressed are those of the author and do not reflect the official policy or position of the publisher or Powerful Women Today.

Copyright Use and Public Information Unless otherwise noted, images have been used according to public information laws.

ISBN: 978-1-7782536-2-1 EBook

ISBN: 978-1-7782536-1-4 Paperback

CONTENTS

PREFACE

W hat's your mission possible?

When someone tells you that you can't do something, is your first instinct to agree with them and wilt like a sun-deprived flower, wondering how you could ever have set such pie-in-the-sky and downright silly goals for yourself?

Or do you immediately feel the defiance welling inside you like hot popcorn kernels in the microwave bursting in the bag and you find even more resolve to accomplish what you have set out to do?

I wish I could say that I've only ever been like popcorn. But the truth is, shrinking violet has always been the safer option for me. Until now.

One morning, an idea woke me up with a start (and I am not a morning person). It told me that I could help women entrepreneurs in their first 5 years of business avoid the common mistakes and reach heights they had only ever dreamed about by creating THE MANUAL of successful entrepreneurship. To make it so rich in value, I would curate a group of brilliant women who could all speak their expertise. This book would have benefited me back when I was starting.

My inner voice immediately told me this was way too lofty a goal. I didn't even need to share the idea with outside naysayers. I was capable of shutting the idea down and saying, 'Why would anyone want to be part of this book project? Just forget it.'

But I couldn't shake it.

So, with severe trepidation, I put my faith and trust in this mission to help women entrepreneurs. And sure enough, 12 brilliant women have put their faith and trust in the mission and joined the journey with me.

Mission Possible: Successful Women Entrepreneurs Sharing Step-By-Step How to Become One is a labor of love and a treasure trove of guidance for female entrepreneurs in the first 5 years of business.

We are moms to fur babies and humans, wives, partners, sisters, and daughters who understand that you should not have to go it alone.

We are here to help your business grow and become your Mission Possible.

MISSION POSSIBLE

Introduction

Missions that became not only **Possible** but both a **Reality** and a **Success**.

Mission Possible #1: Breaking Down Obstacles

Thoughts become reality. Melanie invites us to imagine what your life would be like if there were no obstacles in your way to achieving exactly what you want for yourself. The air you breathe will be fresher, filling your lungs with hope. You will feel a bubbling up of excitement within you as you sit down at your computer to begin your workday, coffee in hand and favorite candle lit, because you will know your desired destiny is possible. But just like it takes a village to raise a child, you definitely do not want to go it alone on your entrepreneurial journey.

Mission Possible #2: Your Health Is Your Wealth

Radical Change sometimes begins as Unexpected Radical Change. Gina's Story: My company had just announced a restructuring. I didn't expect to be impacted until the evening before when the only other manager left in our division called me and said, "Do you think they are going to let us go tomorrow?" First thing in the morning, the email arrived. Inviting me to a meeting with my boss and the VP of HR. I knew the end was coming. A part of me was grateful. At the time, I was worn out, exhausted, and depleted mentally and physically after spending years working extreme hours and traveling weekly. My personal life was in shambles, due to a long and dysfunctional marriage. I didn't have time to deal with any of it because I was drained by work.

Mission Possible #3: ~~Mid~~LIFE Without Crisis

Realizing the ladder was against the wrong wall and doing something about it. For Carolina, it was the courage at age 40 to awaken her Emotional and Financial Independence. *"You were a good mom until you hit a ~~midlife~~ crisis,"* my son once told me. He was 14 at the time and clearly either had heard someone say it, or it had been said about me to him. It hit me like a bucket of

9

freezing water, rendering me speechless; thank God, long enough to notice he was repeating something he did not know the whole meaning of. I was forty when I decided I had enough after 18 years of a non-compatible marriage. I am at peace knowing that during our marriage, we had both been good and bad; we had both been right and wrong. That being said, one thing I was 100% sure of at that moment was a) I was not in *midlife*, and b) I was certainly not in crisis, quite the opposite. You can say my awakening to the state of my life was exactly that...an *awakening*. I was simply unprepared to live the rest of my life, as comfortable and abundant as it seemed on paper, feeling like this was "it." This was only the beginning...independence also lead me to leave my 1% C-Suite career to start my own business.

Mission Possible #4 Begin How You Wish to End

A Coach Is One of the Best Investments in You and Your Business. For Dortha, her own overwhelm inspired her mission to guide others to start on the right footing. As an experienced business owner, I can say without a doubt that having a coach by your side is crucial for business success. Whether you're an entrepreneur or an executive, I am confident in saying that **there are no shortcuts in business**. However, having someone who has been where you are and can guide you through the ups and downs can make all the difference to shorten the runway for your success. This is not any coach; this is an architect coach. Think about it this way: when you are designing a home, you map out where all of the electrical outlets and other infrastructure go so that you know where everything goes. It is the same for business, and you work with an architect coach so that you know where to put everything, what systems to use, etc. and eliminate overwhelm and frustration.

Mission Possible #5: The Power of Authenticity

Being your unfiltered self in the age of social media. You've likely heard the sayings that "People buy from people first; they buy what you are selling second" or "People buy from people they know, like and trust." When you're a solopreneur or run a small business where you are the face of your business, it's critical that people **see your face** and learn about your mission so they can build that know, like, trust factor.

Whether you are just starting out in your business, or you've been running your company for many years, your face must be visible for others to connect to. And to do that, you must share photos of yourself on your website and on the various social media platforms. And Karianne notes that for some, that can feel absolutely paralyzing. In our current age of social media, where everyone uses filters on both their photos AND the stories they share about their businesses and lives, we feel inadequate and often take on the "why should I post anything" mentality. We compare our REAL lives with others' highlight reels and feel like we aren't successful enough, creative enough, exciting enough, pretty enough...worthy enough.

They say the "fight is won during practice." The first five chapters, personal stories shared by our fearless entrepreneurs, certainly were not an easy start. You can confidently say they were the start before the start.

Melanie Herschorn

Dedication

To my grandma Helen who has been my rock and believed in me even when I didn't or couldn't believe...

To my daughter Deanna for whom the sky is truly the limit...

And to all the women entrepreneurs who are ready to forge their own path...

Thank you for inspiring me and the world with who you are.

Chapter 1
Mission Possible: Breaking Down Obstacles

Imagine what your life would be like if there were no obstacles in your way to achieving exactly what you want for yourself.

The air you breathe will be fresher, filling your lungs with hope.

You will feel a bubbling up of excitement within you as you sit down at your computer to begin your workday, coffee in hand and favorite candle lit, because you will know your desired destiny is possible.

But just like it takes a village to raise a child, you definitely do not want to go it alone on your entrepreneurial journey.

If you have ever made a mistake as an entrepreneur, you're in really good company. I made tons of them with my first business venture as a designer and manufacturer of nursing wear. Above all, my largest error was not gathering a community of mentors and vetted experts around me.

This second time around, as a book marketing strategist for nonfiction and children's book authors (incredibly different industries, I know!) I made a conscious effort to change. That means instead of insisting on doing everything by myself, I have sought out the specialists, joined the networking groups, and built a real community around myself. Because of this, I have seen a stunning improvement, not only in income but also in impact.

> *It is all possible for you too: when you give up your lone wolf status and find your pack. But not just any old pack, people who have done what you are seeking to do and have done it successfully.*

Here's some amazing news: you have already taken an important step toward your success by picking up this book.

Mission Possible is the manual that every woman entrepreneur in her first 5 years of business needs. Think of it as your guide to fulfilling your mission as an entrepreneur. It is your opportunity to learn from 13 successful women entrepreneurs who are experts in their chosen fields–from branding and web design to sales and community-building–and have made their mission possible.

We've taken the road less traveled and are here to offer you guidance that will save you time, money, and keep you from boarding the roller coaster ride that spirals out of control. Although 42 percent of small businesses in the U.S. are owned by women, women-owned businesses still only take in half the average annual earnings of businesses owned by men. It is time to change those statistics.

STANDING OUT FROM THE CROWD

Now let's focus on what could be one of the most important actions toward building a successful business: defining your mission.

Many women entrepreneurs don't stop to think about what their mission-the deep down, reason you get out of bed, how you want to change the world-really is. When asked, they will say "to help women in business make more money" or "to retire my spouse" or "to help people in a way that I would have needed when I was in their shoes."

These are all noble causes. I, too, desire to help women make more money, want to retire my husband, and save people from making the mistakes I did.

But therein lies the problem. If we all walk around saying the exact same thing, how do we stand out in a crowded marketplace?

Sure, our friends and family (maybe) and business besties cheer us on, but our ideal clients and customers won't know why they should work with us over our competition.

In my first job after graduating with a master's degree in journalism, I worked in radio news. As "talent" I was often asked (read: told) to attend station events. The first time I was required to give a speech, I couldn't bear the thought of talking about myself. I was a journalist - we are never supposed to be part of the story.

So, I compiled the stories of the inspirational people whom I had featured in my news reports and shared those:

- The Korean war veteran who'd lost part of his jaw in combat and shared his vivid and chilling memories.

- The brave young boys and girls who had lost a parent or sibling and attended camp for bereaved children.

- The teen, stuck for years in the foster care system, who was adopted by his case worker (she was only 10 years older than he was.)

These stories stay with me to this day. And there's a reason for that.

In centuries past, people sat around fires telling stories to explain natural phenomena. Stories are how we, as humans, learn and remember.

When I first started my marketing business, I struggled with what to share. What makes me special? I would wonder. I'm just another entrepreneur. There was no rags-to-riches story for my business. There was no fiery crash from which a phoenix emerged. It was just a decision I made to start a business because it was tapping on my heart, and it would not stop.

You don't need to have a giant, news-worthy event to be unique though. Your stories and how you share them will differentiate you from everyone else. Your unique experiences, education, and transformation will help you stand out from the crowd when you share them with the world. When you get to the crux of your "why" and you share it in a way that resonates with your audience, that's when the magic happens.

MESSAGING MATTERS

Stories are one piece of an overall marketing strategy to convey what makes you different from your competition: your messaging. Clear messaging will enable you to communicate the benefits of working with you in a way that resonates with your ideal audience and inspires them to take action.

When you are trying to dream up the right messaging, you may begin to feel like you're banging your head against a red brick wall. To stop the pain, you settle on something generic just to get it out there. But all you hear is crickets.

Please know that you are not alone. This happens to nearly every entrepreneur at some point in their journey, and not always right at the beginning either. You are not born knowing how to communicate what makes your offer unique. Plus, being so close to something can make it really difficult to describe it effectively to others.

If you've ever scrolled through Facebook or Instagram, you know that so-called gurus love to post messages like "I just made $14K in two days. Download my exact blueprint below!" When we see these posts our first thought is: *This is what we've been searching for. We now can make $14K in two days, too. It is the answer to all our problems. But wait – is it really the holy grail?*

The truth is these "experts" are using the unsuspecting, newer entrepreneurs to build their email subscriber lists in order to sell you something. They are not actually offering you the silver bullet of business success. Unfortunately, promises like these are everywhere and they are really detrimental to entrepreneurs because they play on our emotions. We may feel envious, not good enough, even desperate.

Cookie-cutter, money-making plans that promise you the world are shiny and exciting. But like any get-rich-quick scheme, there's a lot of smoke and mirrors. Just because it worked for the person who created the blueprint does not mean it will work for us. In fact, chances are, it will not.

Want to know the real way to make sure your business makes money?

It all goes back to your messaging. When you are saying what your ideal audience wants to hear, that is your ticket to success. My mission and my passion are to help those with an important message find their voice and share it with the world. Sometimes I have to pinch myself that this is what I get to do every day.

Here is how to create/update/improve your marketing message to ensure that your favorite client will hear what you're saying and want to work with you.

Step 1: Spell out what your mission is. I don't mean your superficial mission like "I want to help women in business make more money." I mean your deeper mission. Here are some questions you can ask yourself. I recommend writing down the answers as the ideas flow.

- What happened in your childhood or early adulthood that had a deep impact on you?

- Why have you gravitated toward this line of work?

- What inspires you to be better, to do better?

- What gets you out of bed in the morning (besides fur babies or children forcing you to feed them)?

- How do you help people?

Step 2: Get really clear on who you serve.

Maybe you help women business owners, for example. Answer these questions to help you gain clarity about your audience. Are they moms? Where do they live? Are they married? Do they have a single income household? What are their values? What keeps them up at night? What are their hopes and dreams? What do they spend their money on?

Step 3: Do your research.

I know. We aren't in school, and research may not be your favorite thing to do but asking the important questions will not only help with your messaging, it will also save you time and money in the long run.

So often I see business owners throwing spaghetti at the wall to see what sticks with regard to their messaging. One day, they talk about one idea and the next week, they're talking about a completely different idea. Well, do you know what happens to a confused mind? It doesn't buy. Confusion is a business killer.

There is already so much noise in the online space. Do you stop to try to figure out something confusing when you're mindlessly scrolling through your Instagram feed? Doubt it. You keep going, likely never to return. That's why knowing what will resonate with your ideal client is key.

So, when you're doing your market research, start by asking questions of people you think could be your ideal clients.

Step 4: Test it out.

It's ok if your first attempt at messaging does not get the desired result. Marketing is meant to be tweaked. Perhaps something happens in the world that requires you to change the tone so as to be mindful of people's feelings. Maybe you add a new product that offers a deeper solution and you niche down even more. Keep adjusting until it works.

As a recovering perfectionist, I do believe that done is always better than perfect. However, setting it and forgetting it won't serve you if your messaging isn't bringing in new business.

About the Author
Melanie Herschorn

Melanie Herschorn wants to make your book and brand shine. As a nonfiction and children's book marketing strategist for authors, coaches, consultants, and speakers worldwide, she's on a mission to support and empower her clients to build a business with their book as the foundation and to help them share their message with the world. Using her unique combination of entrepreneurship, award-winning journalism and PR experience, Melanie guides her clients to create brand awareness, sell books, and position themselves as subject matter experts. She also loves to provide book marketing tips and interview authors on her YouTube show, AUTHORity Marketing LIVE!

Your Mission Possible: Create captivating captions that really resonate with your ideal audience with this free guide at vipbook.marketing/captions.

melanie@vipbookmarketing.com
vipbookmarketing.com

Gina Smith

Dedication

Dedicated to the hard-working women in my family who came before me and did not have the opportunities I've enjoyed.

Chapter 2
Mission Possible: Your Health is Your Wealth

My company had just announced a restructuring. I didn't expect to be impacted until the evening before when the only other manager left in our division called me and said, "Do you think they are going to let us go tomorrow?"

First thing in the morning, the email arrived. Inviting me to a meeting with my boss and the VP of HR. I knew the end was coming. A part of me was grateful. At the time, I was worn out, exhausted, and depleted mentally and physically after spending years working extreme hours and traveling weekly. My personal life was in shambles due to a long and dysfunctional marriage. I didn't have time to deal with any of it because I was drained by work.

Thankfully, I had a year-long severance which eased my worry, and I decided to take some time off just to breathe and get in touch with myself, sleep, and catch up with all the medical appointments I constantly canceled and rescheduled. I was in terrible shape, overweight, sluggish, and disconnected from myself and others. For so long, I had been numbing with work and wine.

In this space, I decided to change how I lived by first improving my health. That meant making a commitment to proper nutrition, reducing consumption of wine and other alcohol, figuring out a workout protocol, reconnecting with myself through journaling, meditation and prayer, and reconnecting with friends and loved ones. It would take longer to address the marital issues.

My perspective on work changed and I was no longer willing to allow it to be the thing that drove everything else about my life. I decided on boundaries I would set for what I would do moving forward by putting my work in its right place. I wanted a fuller, more satisfying life.

> *My perspective on work changed and I was no longer willing to allow it to be the thing that drove everything else about my life.*

Now that I've exited my corporate career and am building my own business as a Coach and Trusted Advisor, I am committed to not recreating the patterns I lived in so long. This happens with so many women who make the shift from working for others to working for themselves. The price of freedom shouldn't be your health and wellbeing. You can make Your Health Your Wealth.

Here is why this is important:

- You are the strongest asset for you and your family.

- We have accepted overextension as a way of life. The grind mentality is not healthy.

- 50% of adults report being consistently exhausted because of work.

- In 2018 the CDC said, "long-term and unresolvable burnout is a major health concern."

- What happens if you become ill from lifestyle disease and can't take care of your responsibilities in creating and running a business?

I created the W.E.A.L.T.H. formula for a group of entrepreneurs using the word wealth as an acronym. The formula is simple and practical.

The W.E.A.L.T.H. Formula

Whitespace

Eating Well

Activity

Love & Connection

Time Management

Hydration

Whitespace is uninterrupted time in silence to think and dream. In our rapidly moving world, it is rare and difficult to find silence. We don't value taking deliberate time to think and dream. It seems worthless because we are not "doing" anything.

Creating this time for yourself is of the highest value. When you fail to do this, your day is run by moment-to-moment urgency.

How can you carve out and plan in your calendar a time and place where you can allow yourself to sit in silence? I know it's uncomfortable because we are not accustomed to silence. Everywhere we go there is noise, music playing, the blaring of television screens. Where can you create this space for yourself?

I recommend you have something to write in, a beautiful journal comes to mind. I have a very specific journal and pen I use to write. The texture of the paper and smoothness of the pen are important sensory elements. This isn't a time to use electronic media. There is a specific connection created between your brain and your heart when you write it out on paper versus typing into a phone or computer.

Use this time to clear your mind, reflect on relationships and consider the larger strategic questions of your life. Allow yourself to sit with the discomfort you feel in silence. Once you block out all the distracting noise you allow space for those feelings and thoughts you've not been noticing.

Start small with 10 minutes of time and gradually build up. You will discover the value of Whitespace as you practice it regularly at least once a week. There is gold in this silence.

Eating Well your body and brain require proper nutrition to function optimally. I am not a nutritionist but I am a certified Health Coach trained in its fundamentals. Do you know that what you eat is one of the most important decisions you make?

In our market and profit driven world there is a popular diet or way of eating promoted every year. Now we're back to the Mediterranean Diet that was the "it diet" about 25 years ago. These recommendations sell lots of books and products. Diet culture is particularly harmful to women creating poor nutritional habits and eating disorders.

The truth is human beings require a balance of Protein, Carbs and Fat at each meal to maintain optimal health. These three elements can be found in various combinations. Eating fresh whole foods should be the foundation of your nutrition.

Avoiding and eliminating as much processed food as possible is crucial.

How you eat is equally important. Are you taking time to allow your five senses to experience the food you eat? Are you eating standing up? On the run? In the car? If you are you are robbing yourself of a full experience. Science says it takes 20 minutes for the brain and the gut brain to communicate satiety.

Are you eating with others? The vibe and community that happens over a shared table helps us slow down, connect and eat well.

Activity our bodies were designed to move. Motion is lotion. The gift of technology has a downside in that most of us are sedentary many hours of the day. As business owners we may still find ourselves sitting in front of a computer screen for hours each day. You've heard the saying, "sitting is the new smoking." Sitting for too long increases your risk of chronic health problems such as heart disease, diabetes and some cancers.

I'm an athlete. I love working out and tackling challenging sports even at the age of 67. I understand everyone is not like that. You don't have to be a hard charging athlete. Can you plan in your day just 30 minutes of activity where you are getting your heart pumping and your body moving?

Here are some ways to move your body:

- Walking

- Yoga

- Swimming

- Cycling

- Strength Training

- Dancing

The important thing is to choose something you find fun, energizing and easily accessible so you will make it a habit.

Love & Connection are essential to health and wellbeing. Just this year (2023) the Surgeon General declared an "epidemic of loneliness" in our country. Connectedness to other human beings is essential to our physical, mental, and societal health.

Have you known that person who is working so hard to provide for the family and ultimately loses them because they ignored the importance of Love & Connection?

How are you creating and maintaining Love & Connection in your life? Do you have a variety of connections in family, friends, and professional connections? Do you have a person or core group of people who you can be completely transparent and real with?

You need to intentionally nurture and care for your relationships. In our busy world, if you leave it to chance, it may never happen. It might seem contrived at the beginning, but intentionally schedule time with your significant other and children where you are 100% present and engaged. Do the same with friends. Leave your devices behind and learn to connect wholeheartedly.

Time Management is really about you managing yourself within time. It's about you deciding how you are going to use your time. I often hear people say, "I don't have time..." The truth is we all have time, and we are all deciding how to use it.

Here are some ways you can manage yourself in time.

- Identify your Top 5 Priorities and these should inform how you decide to use time.

- For heaven's sake, use a calendar. I'm often surprised by professionals who are not using a calendar to manage themselves in time.

- Complete a weekly calendar review at the beginning or end of the week. Are you honoring your Top 5 or is your time being given to the unnecessary and unplanned?

- Are you honoring your yes and your no. "No" is a powerful tool to manage yourself in time.

- Are you programming breaks in your day so that you are not simply rushing from one thing to another?

- Are you allowing realistic time for tasks, meetings and travel?

It's not about managing the time. It's about managing YOU.

Hydration our bodies are 60% water. Essential organs like our heart and brain are 75% or higher. Drinking water daily is crucial for many reasons: to regulate body temperature, keep joints lubricated, prevent infections, deliver nutrients to cells and keep organs functioning properly. Being well-hydrated also improves sleep quality, cognition and mood.

Feeling foggy? Can't sleep well? Stiff and sore? A simple solution may be proper hydration. It's recommended you drink half your body weight in water daily. I like to recommend people drink "wake up" water by pounding 16 oz. of water when you awaken. It gives you a great energetic charge and wakes you up.

Juices, soda, caffeinated drinks, and alcohol all have adverse health effects. Some of these liquids are diuretic and help you dehydrate.

I recommend you find a water vessel that you love. I have a clear cup I purchased at Starbucks years ago. I know it holds 24 oz of water and it helps me visualize and track my progress. We have so many choices now.

If you're not hydrating properly now, you can begin with small steps adding more ounces of water as time goes by until you are at half your body weight. You will begin to see and feel the difference proper hydration makes.

You can make Your Health Your Wealth with these six simple strategies. We often try to do it all at once. Don't do that to yourself. Choose one area at a time. Take small steps along the way on this journey to making Your Health Your Wealth.

About the Author
Gina Smith

If you're anything like me, you've come to realize that success in life isn't necessarily what we think it is. You see, I know what it's like to be caught in the corporate success trap, to be burned out, to feel viscerally that my health is depleting, to know that I'm missing out on family events, sacrificing social engagements and the ability to form deep relationships with others. If you relate to that, then you're in the right place and you might want to read on.

The thing that kept me most trapped was the fact that I was the major wage earner. Not only did this place me in a different position to my partner but it also put an imbalanced level of responsibility on my shoulders. I felt that I couldn't transition to another career or lifestyle. It's a double bind.

What I now do is help other professional women like me to make the transition in a safe, measured, and playful manner. We work together in a way that doesn't compromise your present moment safety for the sake of a better life. We work together to create a better life so you can thrive personally in the midst of success.

I've been coaching all of my life in one way or another. I recently retired from 30 years in healthcare with a number of disciplines, Human Resources, Operations, Sales and Sales Leadership. I spent most of my career with Cardinal Health, a Fortune 20 company, later Owens & Minor and B. Braun Medical, Inc. I've spent years developing team members and contributing to business growth throughout my career.

Now, I get to pursue my passion for helping women full time as a Coach, Consultant and Trusted Advisor. I'm a certified Health Coach and Master Transformational Coach. A U.S. Air Force veteran, I hold a M.A. in Human Relations and management from Webster University in St. Louis, MO.

I'm an athlete who enjoys cycling, swimming, walking, strength training and the occasional triathlon. An art lover, I love discovering and collecting original art. I'm a foodie, wine lover and cook. I'm single and live in Phoenix, AZ.

Your Mission Possible: As a woman in business are you experiencing overwhelm and exhaustion? Have you adopted the grind culture leaving yourself depleted? How long can you keep going down this path? Your Health is Your Wealth provides 6 practical steps that help you change the pattern and make Your Health Your Wealth, so you are thriving not just surviving.

ginarena05@gmail.com
www.ginarsmith.com

Carolina M. Billings, Ph.D. (C), MA–IS

Dedication

To my son Charlie:

My vision, mission, purpose and reward.

*Aspiring to make you proud
is my eternal Mission Possible.*

Photo credit: Pheasant Lane Photography

Chapter 3
~~Mid~~LIFE Without Crisis

Owning the Empowerment, confidence, and
experience that inner power can bring.

---

cri·sis

noun

A time of intense difficulty, trouble, or danger.

"the current economic crisis"

Similar: catastrophe calamity cataclysm emergency disaster predicament plight mess dilemma

A time when a difficult or important decision must be made. (Ding, Ding, Ding)

"When the crisis came, she does not appear to have hesitated."

Similar: critical point decisive point turning point crossroads critical period crux climax climacteric culmination height head moment of truth, zero hour, point of no return Rubicon Crunch.

"You were a good mom until you hit a midlife crisis" my son once told me.

He was 14 at the time, and clearly either had heard someone say it, or it had been told about me. It hit me like a bucket of freezing water, rendering me speechless; thank God, long enough to notice he was repeating something he did not know the whole meaning of. I was forty when I decided I had enough after 18 years of a non-compatible marriage. I am at peace knowing that during our marriage, we had both been good and bad; we had both been right and wrong. That being said, one thing I was 100% sure of at that moment was a) I was not in *midlife*, and b) I was certainly not in crisis, quite the opposite. You can say my awakening to the state of my life was exactly that...an *awakening*. I was simply unprepared to live the rest of my life, as comfortable and abundant as it seemed on paper, feeling like this was "it."

Being a good mom-make that the best mom I can be-had always been and will always be the most important goal, value, and purpose in my life. I am glad my son said what he did, as it made all the subsequent days of my life 100% on point and purpose. Empowerment through reclaiming your life is a thing. As I am on the eve of completing my Doctoral Dissertation and have the most fabulous respectful relationship with my roommate, aka son (he thinks we are ...) I know without a shadow of a doubt that it was the right decision to make for me and seeing how things have turned out for my son, I know I do right by him every day.

> *Being a good mom-make that the best mom I can be-had always been and will always be the most important goal, value, and purpose in my life.*
> *I am glad my son said what he did, as it made all the subsequent days of my life 100% on point and purpose. Empowerment through reclaiming your life is a thing.*

Ladies, we all have our fair share of existential ponderings and hormonal roller coasters. Sure, we've come a long way in smashing glass ceilings and fighting gender biases, but that doesn't mean we're immune to feeling lousy. So, what if we have more opportunities and better equality now? It doesn't erase the fact that sometimes we're overwhelmed and furious. Let's face it; the odds are stacked against us.

Why label it as a crisis? Reaching a milestone in your life is whatever you want it to be.

Can it not just be a fabulous midlife adventure? Some might argue it's all a myth, but the truth is, that many of us experience these roller-coaster emotions at various stages of our lives, not just when we hit the middle mark. It's not a diagnosable condition, but it's part of the emotional whirlwind that can accompany other mental health challenges. Weight changes, sleep disturbances, relationship shifts, and work struggles can all be signs that we're navigating this crazy journey.

So, what are the 15 steps for this grand adventure?

It all starts with the four foundations.

Mission+Vision+Purpose+Reward

It often starts with a trigger or a major life event but can also stem from feeling disconnected or dissatisfied with reality. Denial and anger may rear their heads, followed by constant rumination or impulsive behaviour. The stress of it all might bring us down to a low point. But fear not; with time and support, we can reach a place of acceptance and resolution.

A midlife ~~crisis~~ *adventure* is about realizing we're halfway through this wild ride called life. It's when we question our identity, purpose, and the choices we've made. Deep reflection becomes our companion, urging us to ponder who we are and who we want to become. And hey, if we're going to hit this milestone, let's do it with style!

But how long does this adventure usually last?

Well, that's up to us. We can wallow in it or use it as a catalyst for change. Let's find the root of our feelings, create healthy routines, and shift our perspectives. We can move forward and embrace the satisfaction of our later years.

Now, let's talk about what causes this thrilling midlife ride. Biological changes and shifts in relationships and responsibilities play a big role. Loneliness, uncertainty about our identity, and milestone birthdays can also spark this journey. Life throws curve balls like increased stressors, hormonal shifts, relationship struggles, and career disconnect. But remember, a midlife crisis is often a sign that we crave purpose and meaning. It's an opportunity to evaluate our actions and goals, ensuring they align with our values.

Ah, the signs of this marvellous adventure!

The signs are real, important and personal. From increased depression to deep existential questioning, our emotions can run wild. Sleep troubles, weight changes, and boredom or apathy may accompany us on this journey. We may yearn for the past or desire physical changes to feel younger. Overwhelm, emotional volatility and physical pain can be constant companions. Even our menstrual cycle may play its part. It's all part of the ride; we're here for it!

What is universal about the signs is their meaning,

We have arrived at a place to stop and decide.

Does any of this sound familiar?

- Increased "crossover stressors" from multiple life roles.

- Hormonal changes related to perimenopause or menopause.

- Feeling lonely in their marriage or relationship.

- Identity changes (i.e., identity crisis).

- Loss of fertility.

- Regret about not having children.

- Relationship concerns like divorce.

- Family changes like empty nest syndrome.

- Death of loved ones.

- Caregiving for aging parents.

- Caregiving for children.

- Adult children returning home.

- Career disconnect or apathy.

- Worries about leaving behind a "legacy."

> *Fear not, my fellow adventurous Darlings! We can navigate this life escapade with grace and resilience.*

15 STEPS TO AWAKEN YOUR EMOTIONAL AND FINANCIAL INDEPENDENCE

Whether you choose to work on one specific area of your life, each area of focus does not exist in a vacuum. One of the biggest reasons we think we self-sabotage, which is a very negative thought process, can simply be that we are trying to build one room in a house without considering how it fits within the whole design both structurally and holistically.

The Three Cap Stones

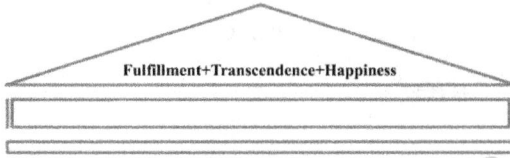

Fulfillment+Transcendence+Happiness

The Eight Pillars of Wellness & Success

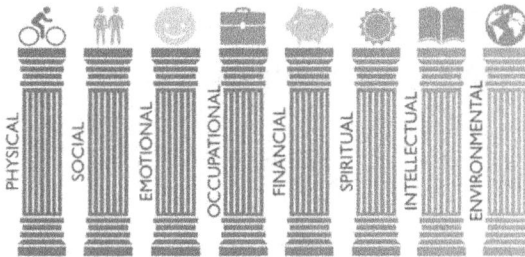

PHYSICAL · SOCIAL · EMOTIONAL · OCCUPATIONAL · FINANCIAL · SPIRITUAL · INTELLECTUAL · ENVIRONMENTAL

The Four Foundations

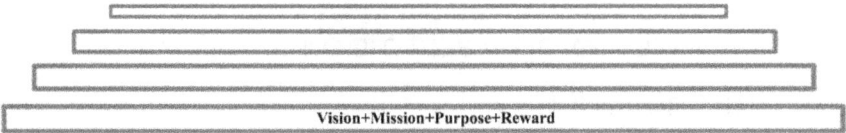

Vision+Mission+Purpose+Reward

The biggest myth in life is that we have time in the future. The only time we have to be our best selves is now.

It's important to reflect deeply on the next set of questions, independent of outside context:

Are you happy?

What are your goals?

How urgent are they?

What do you value? How do your goals align with what you value?

What does success look like? Do you know an example of someone who has achieved something similar to what you aspire to do?

What are your passions?

What is your life purpose?

What are you prepared to do to feel that you are the guiding force in your life?

What are you prepared to say no to?

What are you prepared to say yes to?

66

"Say yes and you'll figure it out afterwards." – Tina Fey

Why are we doing this with pen and paper?

A written goal brings clarity and focus. It gives you direction. And by rewriting your goals, you not only reaffirm what your goals are. You may also find new insights that bring more clarity and focus to your goal and life.

- Writing things down helps you record everything that has your attention.

- Writing things down helps clear your mind.

- Writing things down helps clarify your goals, priorities, and intentions.

- Writing things down helps keep you motivated.

- Writing things down helps you recognize and process your emotions.

- Writing things down encourages daily progress.

- Writing things down enables a higher level of thinking, and therefore, more focused action.

- Writing things down develops your sense of gratitude.

"When you write down your ideas you automatically focus your full attention on them. Few if any of us can write one thought and think another at the same time. Thus, a pencil and paper make excellent concentration tools."

One thing a lot of very successful self-improvement writers – Anthony Robbins, Brian Tracy, Zig Ziglar and so on – go on and on about is the importance of having written goals.

So, get comfortable, breathe deep and let's get started. This is your Before. Do not read ahead. Paint me a picture. On a scale from 1 to 10 tell us (you and me) honestly how do you feel...

How do I feel when…	1	2	3	4	5	6	7	8	9	10
I wake up feeling happy										
I look at myself in pictures										
I put my clothes on										
The phone rings										
I check my emails										
I check my social media										
I visit my family										
I get together with friends										
I tell people about my job										
I tell people about my dreams										
I check my bank account										
I open my bills										
I get into my car										
I think of God or Creator										
I pray/meditate/dream										
I think of love for self										
I think of love for others										
I feel loved										
I think of all that I am now										
I think of all I can be										
I think of all I can achieve										
I think how others must see me										
I think how I see myself										
I think how I see my partner										
I think he/she sees me										

So, let's get moving, embrace the change, and reframe it as a midlife movement! And don't forget to bring others along for the ride. Sharing our experiences with them can strengthen ours.

About the Author
Carolina M. Billings Ph.D. (C), MA-IS

Carolina Billings, Ph.D. (C), MA-IS, is an academic researcher and social impact entrepreneur with 15+ years of Executive Leadership experience in Digital Marketing, Business Development with a focus on Intellectual Property and AI Integration, Communications, Branding, Human Resources and Finance.

Carolina is the founder of Powerful Women Today, a boutique accelerator for success. An ecosystem for empowering and optimizing women's status and lives through Thought Leadership, Visibility, Impact and Legacy.

Her Doctoral Dissertation: *The Impact of Artificial Intelligence Chatbots and Marketing Aggregates on Women Entrepreneurship Generation X and Baby Boomers*, is a substantial piece of scholarly work that contains a significant contribution of new knowledge and literature in the field of Digital Marketing and Entrepreneurship. The results and an analysis of the original research and peer-reviewed papers have been and continue to be published.

Her Boutique Management Consulting Firm comprises elite experts championing women's growth. Her **#1MillionWomenChallenge** aims to positively impact 1 Million Women to bring awareness to end violence against women, strengthen mental health, and end financial dependency.

She is a leader with global impact who Champions and Empowers Women's Emotional and Financial Independence. She is proud of her adoptive home in Canada and her Hispanic heritage. She is a highly active JEDI advocate championing of Social Justice, Diversity, Inclusion and Equity.

Your Mission Possible: Awaken your Emotional and Financial Independence with Powerful Women Today's 15 Steps to Claim Your Power, Create Your Optimal Self and Build the Life of Your Dreams. Realign Your Mission, Vision and Purpose for a life of Happiness, Transcendence and Fulfillment. Giveaways:www.powerfulwomentoday.com/swagbag Win a Feature Spotlight on Powerful Women Today's Magazine and share your Mission Possible. Win a success call with Carolina https://form.jotform.com/PowerfulWomenToday/win-a-success-call-with-carolina

carolina@powerfulwomentoday.com
https://www.linkedin.com/in/carolinabillings
www.powerfulwomentoday.com

Dortha Hise, BSc, BA,
C. Graphic Design

Dedication

---

*To every coach I've collaborated with
over the years: thank you.*

Chapter 4
Begin How You Wish to End

A Coach is One of the Best Investments in You & Your Business

As an experienced business owner, I can say without a doubt that having a coach by your side is crucial for business success. Whether you're an entrepreneur or an executive, I am confident in saying that **there are no shortcuts in business**. However, having someone who has been where you are and can guide you through the ups and downs can make all the difference to shorten the runway for your success.

This is not any coach; this is a **Business Architect Coach**. Think about it this way: when you are designing a home, you map out where all of the electrical outlets and other infrastructure go so that you know where everything goes. It is the same for business, and you work with an architect coach so that you know where to put everything, what systems to use, etc. and eliminate overwhelm and frustration.

A business Architect Coach can provide a fresh perspective, offer valuable insights, and help you navigate the business's complexities. They can help you set goals, develop strategies, and identify areas for growth, all while supporting your dream and helping you to maintain accountability for your actions. Most importantly, a good coach can help you identify blind spots and overcome obstacles that may hold you back.

A business coach can provide a fresh perspective, offer valuable insights, and help you navigate the complexities of running a business.

Here are some reasons why having a coach is so important in business:

Objectivity - When you're in the trenches of the day-to-day of running your business, it can be difficult to see the forest for the trees. You may be so focused on all of the hats you wear in your business, while also meeting clients, and putting out fires that you lose sight of the bigger picture. A coach can provide an objective vantage point on your business. They can help you see things you may have missed, identify new opportunities, and offer solutions to challenges you may be facing.

Guidance & Mentorship - Starting and growing a business can be a lonely and isolating experience. Having a coach can provide you with guidance, support, and mentorship as you navigate the ups and downs of your day-to-day activities. A coach can share their own experiences and offer advice on overcoming challenges and how to achieve your goals more quickly. They can also provide motivation and inspiration when you're feeling discouraged or stuck.

Accountability - One of the most important roles a coach can play is that of an accountability partner. I have found that when I collaborate with a coach, I'm more likely to stay on track and follow through on my commitments. A coach can help you set realistic (that doesn't mean they aren't lofty) goals and create a plan of action to achieve them. They can also hold you accountable for your actions and help you stay focused on what's important. Don't get me wrong – I'm a huge proponent of personal accountability – and always believe that everything starts there.

Skill Development - Running a successful business requires a wide range of skills, from marketing and sales to fiscal management and leadership. A coach can help you develop or hone these skills and provide training and resources to help you grow and improve. They can also offer feedback and guidance to help you refine your skills and become more effective in your role.

Overcoming Obstacles & Limiting Beliefs - Many entrepreneurs, business owners, and executives struggle with limiting beliefs and self-doubt which holds them back from achieving their dreams, goals, and realizing their full potential. A coach can help to identify these limiting beliefs and work through them with you to overcome obstacles and achieve your goals. In some cases, depending on the coach, they can also provide emotional support and help you build the confidence you need to succeed.

Network Building Opportunities - Building a relationship with a coach can also open doors to valuable opportunities to build and grow your network. A coach may have connections in your industry or field and can introduce you to potential partners, clients, or mentors. They can also help you build your network and connect with other professionals who can offer support and guidance.

Improved Decision-Making - When you're running a business, you're faced with countless decisions every day. Having a coach can help you make better, more informed decisions. They can offer insights and advice based on their own experiences and help you weigh the pros and cons of different options. As I mentioned at the start of this chapter, having someone who has navigated the areas you might be struggling with can shine the spotlight on things to carve an easier path, with a shorter runway to success.

Increased Productivity - A coach can also help you increase your productivity and efficiency. They can help you prioritize your tasks, set achievable and stretch goals, and create a plan of action to achieve them. They can also offer time management strategies and tips to help you work smarter, not harder. In addition, you may also consult your coach about delegating certain tasks in your business. You might be amazed to learn all the ways that you could be outsourcing things in your business, which frees up your time and allows you to focus on the things that only YOU can do, or what I call your zone of genius.

A Different Perspective - Working with a coach can also give you a different perspective on your business. They can help you see things from a different angle and challenge your assumptions and beliefs. This can help you break out of old habits and thought patterns and open up new opportunities for growth and innovation.

Improved Communication Skills - Communication is essential in business, and it is not always easy to communicate effectively or clearly. A coach can help you improve your communication skills, both internally and externally. They can help you develop strong relationships with your team, stakeholders, and improve your ability to communicate your vision and goals.

Personal Growth - Collaborating with a coach can also help you grow as a person. They can help you develop your emotional intelligence, build your confidence, and become a more effective leader. They can also help you identify your strengths and weaknesses and develop a plan to overcome personal or professional challenges you may be facing.

Now that we've covered the importance of having a coach in business, let's turn to options for finding the right coach for you.

The list below is in no way meant to be an exhaustive list; it is however meant to serve as a starting point for you to begin your journey. At the end of this chapter, I've included a downloadable resource with a list of questions to ask yourself and your potential coach that can serve as a guide on this journey.

Experience & Expertise - When selecting a coach, look for someone who has experience and expertise in your industry or field. Have they achieved the things you are seeking to do? Look for a successful track record as well as whether they can offer valuable insights and guidance based on their own experiences. It is also important to assess whether they understand the challenges and opportunities in your industry or field. Something else to consider is whether or not it matters to you if they are an accredited coach. There are a lot of coaches in the marketplace and finding one who aligns with your values, business needs, opportunities for growth, etc. are all factors to consider.

Chemistry & Compatibility - It is important to find a coach who you have good chemistry with and who you feel comfortable working with. You ought to be able to communicate openly and honestly with your coach and feel confident that they have your best interests at heart. Look for someone supportive, encouraging, and empathetic. I find it helpful to write a list of the qualities and characteristics I want in a coach when I am seeking a new coach.

Coaching Style - It is likely that nearly every coach out there has different coaching styles, so it's important to find someone whose style aligns with your needs and preferences. Some coaches may be more hands-on and directive, while others may take a more collaborative approach. Look for a coach who can adapt their style to your needs and goals. I find it helpful to assess what I'm seeking coaching for and match that to the style in the coach I'm looking for.

Availability & Accessibility - You want a coach who is accessible and available when you need them. Inquire about their availability and how often you can expect to meet or communicate with them. Ask whether you can reach them between sessions (where the magic happens in coaching) via email or messenger or text message, etc. It also may be important to consider their location if you are seeking in-person coaching. With so many coaches working virtually now, it may not be an issue, however, it is worth mentioning.

Reviews & Testimonials - Before selecting a coach, it is imperative to do your research and read reviews and testimonials from other clients. Ask for referrals from other business owners or professionals in your network.

Once you've found the right coach, it's important to establish clear expectations, set boundaries, and identify goals for your coaching relationship. Your role in this relationship cannot be underestimated. You will need to be prepared to invest in yourself, invest time and effort into your coaching program to maximize your results.

About the Author
Dortha Hise, BSc, BA, C. Graphic Design

Dortha L. Hise is an International Bestselling Author, Founder and Chief Overwhelm Solver of Pretty Smart Virtual Services, a full-service coaching and project management firm specializing in rescuing clients from overwhelm. She is also the Director of Adventure at Summit to Your Success, a choose-your-own-adventure-focused healing technique where she helps others to learn about the healing power of nature. Dortha loves helping her clients to choose their adventures by freeing them up from their to-do lists.

After enduring multiple devastating personal losses, Dortha also lost her voice literally. She thought it was a simple case of laryngitis or bronchitis...as it turns out, it was not simple... She was diagnosed with a neurological condition called Abductor Spasmodic Dysphonia ("AB SD"). AB SD prevented Dortha from using the phone or speaking normally or being easily heard in a room with a lot of ambient noise. While this presented challenges to Dortha, she is grateful for this experience as it has heightened her sense of hearing, most importantly, her ability to listen deeply.

Always the positive thought leader, Dortha remained a high achiever through circumstances that would have knocked many down without feeling overwhelmed. She understood the mindset of high achievers fully and how to optimize their businesses for maximum performance, however, she observed that the overwhelm did not always go away.

After a 3-day backpacking trip in 2015, she fully experienced the healing power that nature brought to her; she had done it naturally with techniques developed both strategically and intuitively... She set an intention to be open to whatever she was meant to receive on that trip. When she returned home, she understood that to be what expanded her resilience and that the final act of letting go brought the ultimate antidote to overwhelm. Dortha, now a certified coach, teaches others to do the same in her Choose Your Own Adventure Healing Portal bringing about entire mind shifts and personal transformation of those who lead, helping them serve the world at their best.

Your Mission Possible: peace of mind is an outcome, not a goal. I hope you join the amazing clients who have said "yes" to a life without overwhelm and fulfilling adventures. Book a call with me to explore more: https://form.jotform. com/dortha/book-a-call

virtual.dortha@gmail.com

summittoyoursuccess.com

Karianne Munstedt

Dedication

---

*To my clients, for showing the
world their real selves.*

Chapter 5
Mission Possible: The Power of Authenticity

Being your unfiltered self in the age of social media

You've likely heard that "People buy from people first; they buy what you are selling second" or "People buy from people they know, like and trust." When you're a solopreneur or run a small business where you are the face of your business, it's critical that people **see your face** and learn about your mission to build that know, like, trust factor.

Whether you are just starting out in your business, or you've been running your company for many years, your face must be visible for others to connect to. And to do that, you must share photos of yourself on your website and on various social media platforms.

And for some, that can feel paralyzing.

In our current age of social media, where everyone uses filters on both their photos AND the stories they share about their businesses and lives, we feel inadequate and often take on the "why should I post anything" mentality. We compare our REAL lives with others' highlight reels and feel like we aren't successful enough, creative enough, exciting enough, pretty enough...worthy enough.

And then paralysis sets in, and we do nothing. We show up in mediocre photos on our website or social media or we don't even show up at all, and we don't give our clients the opportunity to really see us and get to know us.

> *We compare our REAL lives with others' highlight reels and feel like we aren't successful enough, creative enough, exciting enough, pretty enough... worthy enough.*

I didn't have any photos of myself.

As I was building my own portrait photography business, I looked around and realized that I had no photos of myself. During the past decade, I had put on weight, I didn't feel as though my body wasn't perfect enough, and so I didn't want to be in pictures. I didn't want to invest in photos when I didn't feel great about myself. I didn't want to be judged on how I looked.

But as the face of my business, I knew I needed photos for my website and social media.

I booked a photo session with a photographer who I hoped could take at least one good photo of me. On the day of the photo session, I was filled with so much anxiety. My clothes weren't perfect enough; my body still wasn't perfect enough. The negative voices in my head were on full blast and saying, "Kari, you're too fat to be photographed. Kari, no one wants to photograph you. Kari, who do you think you are?" But still, I knew I needed to do this. So, I took a deep breath, tuned out the negative voices the best that I could, and went for it.

And guess what happened?

I had fun! The photographer made me feel like the most beautiful woman in the world. And when I saw the final portraits of myself, I saw the real me—not the outer me—the me in my soul looking back at me. I saw that I didn't have to have the perfect clothes and the perfect body to exist beautifully in photos, to love the woman who I saw staring back at me. I didn't have to be "perfect" for anyone or at anything, I just had to show up as the real, authentic me, and THAT WAS ENOUGH.

And I knew then that I wanted every woman to feel as though they were enough just as they are. No matter what their bodies looked like, or how "successful" their businesses were, how quirky they were, or how messy their lives were, they matter and have a voice in this world.

Professional photos vs. cell photos.

When we are newer in our business, we think that because we have a cell phone, we can get away with solely using cell phone pictures in our marketing. Cell photos should absolutely be used in your overall social media marketing strategy, but they should not be the only types of photos you use.

Professional portraits inspire confidence, both for yourself AND for your viewers. People who invest in you want to see you investing in yourself. They should be used for your official headshot on your website, social media profile photos, in printed marketing materials, and for speaking engagements.

No matter what stage you are at in your business, you should have a photo portfolio that includes both professional portraits and cell phone photos. It is imperative that you invest in photography right from the start and add this as an annual marketing expense.

If you're in year 1-2 of your business, at a minimum, find a headshot photographer in your area. View their profile to make sure your aesthetic style matches theirs and schedule a call to make sure they are a good fit. Use these headshots on your About Me page on your website, on your business-related social media profiles, and for any speaking engagements.

Try to get a few headshots that show some variety. The rest of your photos can be rounded out with cell photos and stock photos for your website.

If you're in year 3 and beyond of your business, and it's steadily growing, it's now time to invest additional dollars into photography with a branding photo session. This is where you'll get a more robust portfolio of images that show more than what you look like; these images present confidence and power and show more of the personality of the person behind the brand, in a professional manner. Find a photographer that you really connect with, even if they're not in your area. Melanie Herschorn said of her branding session, "My branding photoshoot with Karianne was truly the first time I've felt like a CEO." At this stage in business, branding sessions should take place at least every two years, if not more often.

Cell phone photos are where a deeper connection can be made. They give viewers a glimpse into your life and show things that are important to you, like your hobbies and your family. I know that sometimes cell phone photos feel harder to post because you might not have the perfectly curated home or office, or the right light, or your children might not be in the perfect matching outfits, or you don't have someone perfectly dressing, posing and directing you. Don't let these things hold you back. The professional photos show the polished; the cell photos show the everyday, REAL you. And your viewers absolutely want to see both.

Be REAL.

> "*To be yourself in a world that is constantly trying to make you something else is the greatest accomplishment.*"
> *- Ralph Waldo Emerson*

We only have seven seconds to make a first impression, and having impactful photos is the most instantaneous way to make a strong, lasting connection. Sometimes, your photos might cause a viewer to move on, and that's ok – they weren't your client. But for those who stop and lean into you showing your real self - your unapologetic, authentic, unfiltered self – the viewers who lean into those photos ARE your client and are likely to build a connection with you before they even pick up the phone to call you.

The REAL Framework.

By following the R.E.A.L. framework, you'll find the courage to post cell photos of yourself that will form strong connections with your viewers.

- **R**elease: Take a deep breath. Breath in confidence, courage, and kindness. Hold for four seconds. Breathe out perfection, fear, and comparison. Release the negative feelings from your body. Welcome the positive feelings into your body. Repeat as many times as necessary to be in the best frame of mind before posting.

- **E**mbrace: Embrace your quirks, embrace your double chin, embrace your differences, embrace your messy house, embrace your kids not looking at the camera. Embrace all of what makes you and your life YOURS. "Today you are You, that is truer than true. There is no one alive who is Youer than You." – Dr. Seuss

- **A**uthentic: photos are meant to capture the REAL you...the messiness and all! So, when you post cell phone photos, be sure to keep them 100% authentic. No one, no matter how much they try to filter their lives, has a perfect life. Let go of that thought. Be true to who you are.

- **L**ove: When you are ready to press post, place your hand over your heart and repeat, "I am all love." You are sending your post out into the world with love and inviting those who value your post to receive it in love.

Your social media doesn't have to be anything other than what you want it to be. You don't have to do reels, or dances, or use heavy filters because others are doing it. Whatever you post on social media should feel authentic to you. Trust your intuition. Be you.

In the age of social media, when we see so many filtered photos and stories, it can feel intimidating to share unfiltered photos and stories of our own lives and businesses. It can feel impossible to show up online as our real selves when we compare ourselves to the highlight reels of others. However, if you have an online presence, it is absolutely imperative that you show up in both professional and cell photos on your website and social media. And by following the R.E.A.L. Framework, you'll find the courage to post cell photos of your 100% authentic self, which will help viewers form a deep connection with you and choose to work with you instead of the next person.

About the Author
Karianne Munstedt

Karianne is a portrait photographer and business owner, a speaker, coach and author. She is an artist and nurturer, fiercely motivated by using her talents to make women feel confident, empowered, and whole. As a curvy woman who was very critical of her body, she spent nearly a decade hiding behind the camera, never stepping in front of it out of fear of shame and judgment around her body and choices.

Now, Karianne exists fully not only in photos, but also in business and in life, and inspires women around the world to fully show up as the real versions of themselves as well.

Karianne has received multiple awards for her photography, was named Business Owner of the Year for the Phoenix Chapter of the National Association of Women Business

Owners, and was a recipient of the Athena Valley of the Sun "Lives Authentically" Award. Personally, Karianne is a wife, mommy to a toddler, stepmom to a teenager, and doggy mama.

Your Mission Possible: By following our 4-step framework, you'll find the courage to post photos of your 100% authentic self, which will help viewers form a deep connection with you and choose to work with you instead of the next person. Get the guide here: https://kariannemunstedt.com/stopjudgmentfreegift/

kari@kariannemunstedt.com
kariannemunstedt.com

Stacy Lang

Dedication

To my husband and son, to my amazing team, and to our wonderful clients. Each of you teach me new things about business and myself every day.

Chapter 6
Mission Possible:
Money Mindset

While I help others with their money mindset, I had to tackle my own. As a lifelong people-pleaser, I worked so many hours to get the job done and ensure the client was happy. I was the only person whose happiness didn't seem to concern me.

Coming from a long line of entrepreneurs in my family, I had started several 'side hustles' over the years before officially becoming self-employed in early 2008. As of this writing, I recently celebrated my business's 15th anniversary. When I started the business, it was just a 'side hustle' on top of my regular full-time job in the accounting department of a national homebuilder. I had done contract work with a few local CPAs over the years, helping them out during tax season and preparing returns. I loved the rote-ness of the work - I'd show up, and sit down next to a tower of tax folders with personal documents inside. Then I'd slowly work my way through the stack. As I was working, my thoughts would wander...I would look at the clients' wage income, investments, charitable contributions, and naturally think of my own situation. Over time, I would gravitate towards the more complicated tax returns - a rental property, a small business, how exciting! This just whetted my appetite for working directly with clients, instead of with just their paperwork.

After a few years of contract work, I started to gain some of my own clients. First, it was friends and family, then a few referrals. I had business cards printed and left them at local coffee shops. I joined a local networking group.

All this time, as I was gaining new clients, I wasn't thinking about 'fit,' profitability, or any kind of longer-term strategy. I had low prices, and that was enough to generate new clients. I had my full-time job, with health insurance and retirement benefits, and my side-hustle was just to earn some extra money, fill some time, and expand my skills.

When starting a business, if you have 5 clients, and 20% of them refer a friend, you now have 1 new client. Once you have, say, 20 clients, if 20% of them refer, you now have 4 new clients. 100 clients get you an additional 20. Having low, low prices really attracts bargain-seeking clients! Having a low self-worth and a people-pleasing manner really attracts bargain-seeking, high-maintenance clients!

Over a fairly short period of time, my side-hustle grew to a point where I went to my boss at the homebuilder and asked him if I could reduce my hours down from full-time to part-time. Doing that put me on an hourly wage instead of a salary. and I lost my health insurance and other benefits. As a (at the time) single woman of child-bearing age, this vastly increased my health insurance expense, but with the growing business income I was able to make it work.

In the meantime, I started dating the man who would later become my husband, and the housing industry was starting to struggle. This was somewhere around 2006 - 2007, and I was in my mid-30s. Over the next six months or so, as my client base grew, and with seasonal and year-round contract work with two local CPAs, I was able to leave my, at this point, part-time job at the home builders, and go full time on my own. I finally had the time-freedom and flexibility to manage my own time! (Or did I?)

It's funny how we can start a business in order to gain the flexibility of our time, but all that means is that we end up working (or thinking about work) 24/7. Being able to do the bookkeeping and tax returns for my clients whenever I wanted led to doing the bookkeeping and tax returns seven days a week, and at all hours of the day and night.

It was around this time that I married my husband, who had since left our shared employer and gone to another job. About a year and a half later, just after my 40th birthday, our son was born. My business was around 3 years old, and after I let go of my contract work, I realized that I really needed to make my first hire. This is really where the cracks started to show. You see, I had a full roster of low-paying, high-demand clients, and a toddler, quickly growing into a preschooler. My prices were so low, I really struggled to pay an employee. But hiring was, for me, the only way to scale my business and focus on the work that I loved. More high-value work, directly with my clients, and less document-chasing, administrative tasks that I could easily outsource. What I discovered at that point was, as long as I was willing to pull all-nighters, the work got done, and it didn't really matter how much I charged. Once I had an employee to pay, I had no choice but to raise my prices.

MATH LESSON: 50 monthly clients at $200 per client = $10,000 per month in revenue and working 150 hours a month. If you raise your price just 15%, and charge $230 per month, you can have 15% fewer clients, work 15% fewer hours, and still make the same amount per month! Even if you lose, let's say 10% of your client list (which, chances are you won't), you will still come out ahead in time and money.

Another necessary thing when hiring is to develop your systems and your SOPs. I will let others speak to this area of business, as it's definitely an area in which I struggle, but being able to delegate work to others, and not have to hold every bit of client information, and workflow inside your own head is crucial to scaling and growing your business.

As the years went on, I kept learning more about running a business, managing a team, and I learned more and more about myself, and what I value as an entrepreneur and service provider. As I delegated more to my team (which has now grown to 5 employees), I became a little bit dissatisfied with the type of work I was delivering to clients.

The quality was very good, the prices still fair, and the timeliness of the delivery improved steadily and consistently over time. But I wanted to provide more value to my clients. I was developing a body of knowledge and expertise that I just knew I could be passing along to other business owners. I just didn't have a framework to make that happen.

METHOD LESSON: When you're starting and growing your business, make sure that you have experts in your corner. Whether it's getting your legal contracts laid out (Attorney!), getting your systems and SOPs put together (Fractional Operations Manager!), or knowing how and when to pay yourself, and what tax structure to set up (CPA / Enrolled Agent / Bookkeeper!), and how to plan for profitability (Certified Profit First Professional Accountant, Bookkeeper, or Coach!) gather up, and utilize your advisory team.

This is where the Profit First methodology came in. I was introduced to Profit First, and the other works of Mike Michalowicz in late 2018 by a family member who also owned a business. As soon as I read the book, I knew that this was something I could use to provide a higher level of service to my clients. The premise of the book is simple: every dollar that comes into your business as revenue has a predetermined destination - saving for taxes, paying yourself as the business owner, saving for profit distributions, and only what's left over is spent on your operating expenses. This is a vastly simplified explanation; I highly recommend reading the book: *Profit First: Transform Your Business from a Cash-Eating Monster to a Money-Making Machine.*

In short order, I became a Certified Profit First Professional, and up leveled to a Mastery Level PFP the following year. Using Profit First, as well as other knowledge I'd gained over the 15 years of business, I'm able to not only provide bookkeeping and tax preparation services, but really coach my clients in how to be more profitable.

Mike Michalowicz, with his book Profit First, and other books he has written, strives to "eradicate entrepreneurial poverty."

As I began working with my clients in a more coaching capacity, helping them shift their mindset to profitability also helped me to continue to shift my own. Not only did I need to make sure that I was able to keep up with client workload, and pay my team members, I also needed to make sure that I was getting paid, and not getting burned out of my own business.

To keep good employees, I also needed to factor in vacation and sick time, retirement benefits for them and for myself, and a good work-life balance and flexibility. I needed to make sure that I had a good balance of clients, and at an appropriate price-point to keep my team paid, challenged, happy, and appreciated. I also needed to make sure that the clients were well-served, that they felt valued and that they value us and our expertise, while paying at an appropriate level to keep everyone satisfied and still profitable. And NOT least, to be managing the business that I envisioned when I started, taking home the salary that I deserve, that I feel challenged but not overwhelmed, that I value and am valued by my team and our clients, and that I have the flexibility and time to appreciate my family, friends, and hobbies.

And I and my team apply all of these lessons to the work we do with our clients.

MINDSET LESSON: You don't have to know everything and do everything the right way right out of the gate. It sounds cliché, but it's true - business ownership, like everything else in life, is a journey. You learn, grow, and change over time. It's taken me over 15 years of business, and over 50 years of living to get to this point, and there is still so much to learn!

About the Author
Stacy Lang

Lang Accounting Services is a boutique accounting and bookkeeping agency in the Phoenix area that serves small businesses and their CEOs in bookkeeping, personal and business taxes and the paperwork of starting up a business. We specialize in educating and empowering business owners, so they feel at ease with where their finances are and ready to make decisions in their organization.

We do the hard work, number crunching and research so you don't have to, then stay on top of your books so you can rest assured that you remain financially healthy and ready to grow.

Stacy Lang is a Certified Public Accountant, Mastery Level Certified Profit First Professional and has more than 20 years' experience in the field. She is passionate about helping small business owners take control of their finances so they can make a bigger impact on their family, their future and their community.

Stacy's passion for small business stems from her entrepreneurial family. From her maternal grandfather's cattle ranch to her father's sales firm, her uncle's veterinary practice, and her mother's crafting side hustle, business ownership runs in the veins. Stacy is an accomplished crafter like her mother, and she loves spending time with her husband and son.

Your Mission Possible: Do you struggle with how to be profitable in your business? Do you have questions on pricing your product or service for growth and profitability? And do you struggle with trying to be all things to all people? Why growing your business can be a vehicle for your own personal growth and mindset shifts.

stacy@langaccountingservices.com
www.langaccountingservices.com

Jenny Belanger

Dedication

---

*To my darling daughter, may you always
believe in the power of women and yourself.*

Chapter 7
Mission Possible:
Brand + Website Design

Build a Winning Brand and Website

It's a familiar story in entrepreneurship. A woman becomes a mom, leaves her job, and embarks on starting her own business to balance her desire to stay at home with her baby and work for herself. And for me, I was no different.

When my son was born, I realized that returning to my non-profit marketing job wasn't an option. I had been lucky to have picked up website-building side jobs here and there, but officially launching my website business was a whole new challenge - and it was no easy feat. However, I knew deep down that I had to make it happen.

For several months, I worked tirelessly without seeing any noticeable progress, and there were definitely moments of self-doubt along the way. But what I learned is that when you decide, you have to keep pushing forward, even when it seems like nothing is working. If you stay the course and keep taking action, all those small pieces will eventually come together, and you'll see results.

That's exactly what happened to me. Starting my business was my biggest challenge, but it's now my greatest achievement. Every day, I get to be my own boss, work on creative projects that bring me fulfillment, and collaborate with clients that I adore. And the best part? I get to be there for my family on my terms every single day — whether it's being a guest reader in my daughter's classroom or booking a last-minute trip with the whole family. I am in control of my time, and that's an incredible feeling.

I want to make your entrepreneurial journey a little smoother, so let's talk about two essential elements that every business needs: a brand and a website. These two components are intertwined and work together to establish a strong online presence. Let me break it down for you.

Think of your brand as the cover of a book. It's what catches the reader's eye and gives them an idea of what the book is about. Your brand includes your logo, colors, fonts, and overall visual identity.

Now, think of your website design as the pages and layout of the book. The pages and layout of a book are what allow the reader to easily navigate and understand the content, just as the design of your website should allow your visitors to easily navigate and understand your business. The website design includes the layout, user experience, and functionality that all work together to create a seamless and engaging user experience.

While your logo is an important part of your branding, it's just one element of your brand identity. Your brand encompasses the entire perceptions and experience that people have with your business. From the way you communicate with them to the products and services you offer.

You'll first want to get clear on communicating your value, mission and vision. Understanding what you stand for and why you have your business. Ask yourself: What are your core values? What are your long-term goals? What is the impact you want to make on your industry? Write out a mission statement that encompasses these answers. And think about your vision for the future. How do you want to get there? By understanding this, you can then develop your brand messaging and start communicating with your ideal clients in a way that resonates with them and sets you apart from the competition.

Next, you'll want to develop your visual identity. This includes your brand colors, logo, and typography.

Colors can evoke emotions and create associations, so picking the right colors can help to establish a strong brand identity that resonates with your ideal client. If your brand is energetic and youthful, bright and bold colors like red or yellow may work. If your brand is more sophisticated and elegant, perhaps muted and neutral colors may be more appropriate. The colors you choose should reflect your brand personality and values, and be consistent across all your marketing channels.

When it comes to your logo, first decide on a style. Do you want something modern or minimalistic? Or are you looking for something more traditional and ornate? Not sure what you want? Research your competitors and do some searching on Pinterest. In entrepreneurship, we tend to refine our brand every few years, so start somewhere and remember this is your first logo and it doesn't have to be forever.

And finally, you'll need to choose your typography. If you're a modern and minimalist brand, perhaps a sans-serif font might work best. More traditional? You'll most likely want to go with a serif font. Stick to a clean header font and body font and perhaps add one more for accents, for example a signature or really bold modern font. Whatever you choose, it needs to be legible and easy to read.

A great resource is Etsy or Creative Market for a "brand starter kit." These provide an affordable way to get the foundation of your business settled so you can go on to build your website

and start marketing yourself. Once your brand is in place, it's time to turn to your website.

There is no doubt that every business needs a website, no matter what you sell, services or actual products. Even if people are finding you on social media, you need to have a place for them to find out more information about you and your business. **A good website is like an employee who works for you 24/7 bringing in leads and making you money.** A bad website could be turning people off and costing you a lot in sales.

Many times, people think of their website as a brochure website. Meaning it's just there to showcase what they do. But to me, if it's not producing any leads and making you money, it's not doing its job.

As a business owner, you have to get your website right and it needs to make you money.

The single most important piece of your website is the above the fold on your home page. We're all busy these days and you have less than 3 seconds to capture your visitors' attention.

Immediately upon landing you need to make it clear:

- What you sell
- Why should that matter (how is it going to help them and make their life better)
- How they can do business with you

Visually this looks like two lines of copy and a button. If anything is confusing, the visitor isn't going to know they are in the right place and are going to leave.

Not sure what to write? Here's a simple formula. For the headline, include what you do. For the subheading, share how you improve your client's life. Not sure how to word it? Use a tool with ChatGPT and bounce ideas around. But keep in mind, **clear over clever** always wins.

The second most important is to understand what the overall goal of your website is as in what is the first step in your sales process. That is how to build the customer journey on your website where all roads lead to this action. If you're a service-based business, many times it's to have visitors fill out your inquiry form or schedule a consultation. For creators, it could be to purchase your course or join your membership. Whatever that one goal is, your entire website needs to be built with this in mind and your direct call to action needs to support that. And it needs to be repeated over and over throughout the website. Driving people to that first step. Make it so obvious for people to know what to do.

Practically, these calls to action will show up in the form of buttons throughout your website in each "section". But the most important place to include it will be in the upper right corner of your website in the form of a button. That is your prime real estate and one of the most important places on your website. Ensure that the button in the upper right-hand corner supports the overall goal of the website. You can grab my free resource, The Secrets to a Money-Making Home Page, to see how these strategies can be implemented on your website.

Next let's talk about imagery. Including photos of yourself on your website can make a huge difference in establishing a personal connection with your audience. I know it can be nerve-wracking to put yourself out there, but showing your face on your website can help people feel more connected to you on a personal level. When people see the person behind the business, it can increase the trust and credibility they have in you and your brand.

Not only that but showcasing photos of yourself can also help convey your vision, mission, and style. Your personality and brand can shine through in these photos, which can help you stand out in a crowded online space. It's important to remember that people like to do business with people, and having photos of yourself on your website can help you build a stronger personal brand and connect with your audience. So, don't be afraid to show off who you are!

And finally, remember, when starting it's okay to begin small. It doesn't have to be a complex website — even a single page can do the trick. This is a great way to establish an online presence without needing to invest a lot of resources or have technical expertise. Plus, it's usually more cost-effective too.

The key is to make sure your website, however small or large you decide, looks professional with photos of you and reflects your brand. This will help build trust with visitors, give you credibility, and allow people to learn more about you and your services. The most important part is to make sure your website directs people towards taking action that supports your overall goals.

By following these brand and website tips, you can establish a solid foundation for your business and begin marketing your services to attract ideal clients and increase revenue. So, get out there and do your thing. And most importantly, have fun!

About the Author
Jenny Belanger

Jenny Belanger is the CEO and Creative Director of JennyB Designs, a website design studio. She helps entrepreneurs and small businesses build websites that communicate and connect with visitors and attract their ideal clients.

With a background in non-profit and corporate marketing + communications, she has been designing websites for over 20 years. Jenny understands that building a brand and website can be overwhelming. She strives to simplify the process so that busy entrepreneurs can be proud of their online presence, land more clients, and get back to business. She lives in Massachusetts with her husband, two kids, and dog, and is addicted to her desk treadmill.

Your Mission Possible: Discover the secrets to a money-making homepage - get the guide here: https://jennyb-designs.com/secrets-to-a-money-making-home-page/

jenny@jennyb-designs.com
www.jennyb-designs.com

Hallie Agostinelli

Dedication

This chapter is dedicated to my father,
who taught me that when you are on time,
you are late. That work ethic is a huge
reason I am able to create this business.
Thank you.

Chapter 8
Mission Possible:
Launch Your Offer Confidently

The Accidental Agency Owner

I used to be the worst business owner. As a matter of fact, my current company is my third attempt at entrepreneurship – the first two tries were big flops. Hello, I am Hallie, and I am a recovering perfectionist. I bring up perfectionism here because it was a huge reason why creating a successful business was so challenging for me. I excelled in every other job I had in my long, multi-faceted career. Always being promoted, earning awards, taking leadership roles whenever possible.

But when it came to working for myself, I could not find the right formula. I would forget to invoice clients. I procrastinated on projects. It was embarrassing. I had no idea what I was doing.

I closed my virtual marketing assistant business and went back to work full time at a real estate office as their Operations & Marketing Manager. Three months later, the pandemic was upon us, we went to work from home, and my hours were cut in half. I needed to find a way to pay the bills (since those did not happen to also be cut in half) so I put the word out that I could pick up some marketing work on the side.

Something magical happened. I stumbled upon a group of female online coaches using a method called "launches" to grow their group memberships and they needed a ton of support. I had never heard of a launch before other than when a rocket ship goes into outer space. I quickly learned the process, perfected my own methods, and started running launches as my main source of income.

I made up processes on-the-go. I made my client's success my measure of success. I treated each launch as if it were my only launch. I took imperfect action and made the most of the opportunities in front of me. I also made it a safe place for my team to mess up.

This is how I came to say I built an agency on accident. And shocker - this time it was successful!

I learned more in those first two years than I could have imagined. I saw launches with zero sales, and I saw launches resulting in multiple six-figures. I have learned the ins and outs of how to launch a course or coaching program using a variety of launch methods. The verdict: Launches work! But they do require a solid strategy and consistent plan.

What the heck is a launch?

A launch is a conversion event where you deliver a high-value workshop, often at no cost, to an audience of potential clients. During the event you present an offer to work with you in a coaching program or course.

To give a real-life example, a coach for interior designers has a 12-month group program teaching them how to run a successful interior design firm. Her launch is a free 5-day workshop taking the participants through her signature sales process which promises to show them how to qualify, quote and close good projects.

The feedback we receive on this workshop: attendees say her free workshop is more valuable than other courses that they paid for. It helps the people not quite ready for her paid coaching program to set things in place so that they can be in the future. It builds good will as she serves her community.

The launch workshop is a vital part of the selling process as it sets them up for success and leaves them wanting to experience more of what you are offering.

10 STEPS TO CREATE A WINNING LAUNCH

Supporting over 150 launches with a wide range of results, I have learned a thing or two about what makes a launch successful. Here is the process I personally walk my clients through when they want to create a paid coaching program or course using launches to enroll clients.

PRO TIP: Before you go any further let's talk about "overwhelm". It is easy to read the following 10 steps, go right to the feeling of overwhelm, and not even take the first step forward. I get it. Launching is a simple process, but it is not easy, and it takes a certain time and energy commitment.

Resist the urge to go into task-mode when you read and instead simply consume this information for understanding. When you are ready to act, you can do this one step at a time.

Step 1: Begin With The End In Mind. Spend some time thinking about the offer you are creating and asking if it fits with your life plan. Build a program or course around the life YOU want. Yes, you want to consider the most effective way to get results for your clients, but the right clients find their way to you when you are clear on this.

Step 2: Launch It Before You Build It. If you wait until you create the content, slide decks and recording for every module you are less likely to actually launch it. Prepare your welcome section and first module, then drip out the rest weekly.

You will learn so much about what content they need most so releasing it a little at a time works in everyone's favor.

Step 3: Pick Your Launch Type. I find the Facebook challenge launch creates the most revenue due in part to live teaching and live selling, but you need to pick the one that best suits you. You can always add additional launch methods to your strategy in future years. Options are FB Challenge, Masterclass and Evergreen Webinars.

Step 4: Create the Free Workshop. Teach something that will solve an immediate problem that leads into your paid program or course. Get tactical and be clear in your workshop title and daily topics so they know why this is a must-attend event. This is often a small part of your paid program spread out over the week.

Step 5: Fill the Workshop. You will see a conversion rate of 1.5 - 5% of the people registering for your workshop so you will want to run numbers to see how many registrants you need to meet your revenue goals. 300 registrants is a good number to start. Use Facebook ads to fill launches with an organic lead generation strategy ongoing.

Step 6: Set Up Tech, Collateral & Copy. This is the FUN part! Simple is better and imperfect action is key here – you can always update for your next launch. Use AI to help give ideas for some of the copywriting but always make it your own. You will need to create branded graphics, emails, workbooks, social posts, and sales page copy. Your emails and posts have three purposes: to invite them to register, to invite them to show up to the launch and invite them to pay for your program or course.

Step 7: Put Self-care Routine in Place. Your launch needs you to be well rested, fed and relaxed. Plan out your meals & work outs and delegate what you can. Something unexpected will happen that week so you want to go into the week with a light load. Use meditation or prayer to have a clear, focused mind and release any worry for the week ahead.

Step 8: Deliver the Launch Workshop. This is the moment you have been waiting for! You've worked so hard to plan it all out – focus on enjoying this week and rolling with the punches. Know that however the week goes, it will be perfect. Remember you are the expert in your field and have so much to share.

Be yourself and have FUN!

Step 9: Debrief and Review. Once the dust settles and you have rested up, take a look at your numbers. Don't just look at feelings or gut instincts here, although those are also important. Get your team involved with the conversation. Review conversion rates, show up rates and overall ROI. Discover what worked and what didn't work and celebrate the successes!

Step 10: Rinse and Repeat Your Launch. Yes, you should rinse this launch off and repeat it again. And again. And again. Launching 4-6 times a year is recommended and works well to build consistent revenue. The launch is brand-building and becomes one thing you are known for in the market. Your audience often attends multiple launches before buying - it works!

THE FLIP SIDE OF LAUNCHING

Nothing bugs me more than seeing an online business celebrate their money-making launches without sharing the roller coaster they rode on the way there. It's a wild ride but it can be fun if you put on your best mindset.

Here is the one message I would like you to remember as you head into the launch space:

Almost everything is "normal."

Six-figure launch followed by a five-figure launch? Normal. Facebook ads work one launch and not so well the next? Normal. Deliver the most beautiful open cart transition one launch and stumble over your words the next one? Normal. Tech gremlins at play out of the blue? Normal. Feeling high off of the launch experience one time then dread it the next? Normal.

We know people post highlights only on IG, so remember that as you launch your new program or course. It takes time. Each launch will build on the next. You are never "done" but you will see

119

consistent success over time when you follow the process and take imperfect action.

> **66**
> *You will either get the results you wanted or the lesson you needed.*
> *— James Wedmore*

> **66**
> *The goal is progress not perfection.*
> *— Kathy Freston*

About the Author
Hallie Agostinelli

Hallie Agostinelli co-founded Predictable Profit, an agency serving online coaches and course creators. She helps business professionals turn their vast industry knowledge and expertise into lucrative, valuable online programs. Before starting her own business, Hallie had over 30 years in the traditional workforce, including powerhouse companies Wells Fargo Home Mortgage and BNI, a global networking organization.

Your Mission Possible: To show online coaches and course creators that you can confidently launch an offer on your own or with a small team. The main goal of a launch is to show your audience the transformation they will have when working with you.

To download The Ultimate Launch Checklist visit:https://www.mypredictableprofit.com/checklist

hallie@mypredictableprofit.com
www.mypredictableprofit.com

Aleasha Bahr

Dedication

---

*To my children, the best
negotiators I know.*

*And to all the women who
don't fit in a box.*

Chapter 9
Mission Possible:
Sell Like a Natural

So, you started a business (congrats!) and now you have to sell something - and you might be thinking "don't make me!"

Why can't we just make money by showing up and doing the thing that we're really good at, that's NOT sales?

But being a business owner in the beginning means wearing ALL the hats. And I might be biased but - the sales hat is one of THE most important hats. Because it's directly related to how you will actually make money and keep your business open. So, you can keep doing that thing you love doing with a flexible schedule, no office politics and all the other reasons people start businesses.

My sales career started like many others in corporate. Specifically, I sold digital marketing to small, medium and large businesses. I was lucky in that I was always a natural at sales although I never knew how to explain what I did to someone else (until now). This is something all people who are natural at sales struggle with. When asked "how are you so good at sales?" the answer is usually "well, I don't really sell" - which is wildly unhelpful information for someone trying to learn how to sell.

Since then, I've evolved to be able to articulate it so someone else can replicate the style of "natural sellers" but before that, I simply observed how other people "sold" and adopted any approaches that felt comfortable to me. The result was something custom to me and only me that felt great and worked like a charm.

Inevitably at any company they try to bring in sales trainers at some point. I remember the ego driven, older white men that came in to train us looked like the typical "sales guys" I would never trust, buy from or even want to hang out with. They emphasized "controlling the call," "digging into pain," "bridging the gap," and nothing they said aligned with me. I was seeing good results with what I already did so I decided "yea I'm going to ignore everything, they said and just keep doing what works for me."

Not everyone at our company had that strong of a compass though and these guys were the "experts" our leadership paid to train us and instructed us to follow. So, many started implementing their advice and their sales and confidence plummeted as a result.

That was the beginning of my first realization - sales is not a one-size-fits all - which makes sense. Because is anything in life one-size-fits all?

My second realization was that sales should NEVER feel uncomfortable.

Think of sales strategies like outfits and you're identifying the one that fits your style.

So, you want to "shop" or learn a strategy from someone with a similar style to you.

And don't force yourself to wear something that's not your style!

Because if it feels uncomfortable to you then I guarantee your prospect feels uncomfortable too.

If you've done sales in your previous career, you might feel like you've got this - and it's true that you have a fantastic foundation.

But you'll find that selling yourself can feel... different (there was definitely a learning curve for me).

If you've never done sales before then you might be breaking out in a cold sweat at the thought.

It's not that you didn't realize you would have to sell something when you opened a business but maybe you didn't REALLY think about it. And now that you're faced with it - it can seem like a big, daunting, hairy task.

So, this is typically what happens when a new business owner gets started:

- Do everything except sales related tasks first - set up your website, talk to friends, network, write a blog, set up socials, etc.

- Keep trying to do everything except sales because you don't know how to sell or what to do.

- Eventually, you're no longer able to put off learning sales as an important to-do so you start researching it and you come across a bunch of old, aggressive white guys pontificating on sales and it's every nightmare you imagined.

- But you decide you're going to buck up and put on your big girl pants because if this is what it takes to be a business owner - then you're all in!

- You get a script online or from a sales expert of some sort. It feels weird and unaligned but they say sales is supposed to feel weird and uncomfortable. They promise that after hundreds of repetitions (and rejections) it no longer feels weird.

- You follow the sales script to a tee - no one buys. You dread the calls. It's bringing back the PTSD of every embarrassing school dance rejection you've experienced.

Let me stop you right here and give you some good news.

Scripts typically don't work - it's NOT just you.

The reason they don't work is that humans are unpredictable - and there are TWO of them involved in a sales conversation.

It would be impossible to script every possible scenario. So, what do you do instead?

You create a compass for yourself and hold yourself to it throughout the conversation. And that compass is "selling" based on fit. Don't even think of it as selling actually - think of it as fitting.

And you will be repelling the people who are not a fit as much as you're attracting the people who are a fit. This is what "natural sellers" do and the reason they say, "They don't really sell."

It's because sometimes they tell someone to buy something else because that prospect isn't a fit for what they sell.

Now - the next question is - how do you know who is a fit and who isn't? Well, I can tell you there needs to be more criteria than "they have a working credit card and are willing to pay."

Ask yourself these questions:

1.   What patterns do you notice in people who LOVE working with you and you feel the same? Beyond demographics like age, gender, job, etc.

2.   What patterns do you notice in people who are NOT happy with their results and/or you did not enjoy working with?

Example patterns to look for are:

- Expectations around how available you will be or what deliverables you fulfill.

- Goals for the results they want.

- Products or services they've invested in before.

- Important pieces they have in place already before working with you.

- Challenges they're currently facing.

- Challenges they've already figured out and are no longer facing.

- Budget will always be an important element to consider as well. No need to talk to people who can't afford you (this is for their benefit as much as yours!)

Once you have these criteria broken down, you will reverse engineer your sales strategy around it.

The questions you ask will be designed to uncover whether someone is a fit. And you'll be very honest when someone is not a fit.

You never want to simply say, "Sorry I can't help you - bye." These people can easily come back to work with you later or refer you. And also - karma is a real thing. Instead, offer them another resource that would be a better fit for where they are right now.

Trust is the foundation necessary for a sale to occur and this transparency goes a LONG way in building trust with someone. It's rare someone selling something will tell the other person not to buy from them and it makes it clear you're not just in it for the other person's money.

When someone is a fit, you're going to tell them why. It makes it very easy to transition to the sale and "asking for the business" because if it's a fit, it's a fact and there's no selling involved.

As an example, this could sound like "ok great well your goals and expectations like [list them out] are realistic for the results clients see with me. You also [list the other reasons] which are the things I need to be successful with you. So, let's do it!"

Now of course there are many layers to sales to add on, but this basic foundation helps you more than any script ever will.

Remember, you're not a gross person taking someone's money. You're a mother, sister, daughter, friend - just like the human sitting across from you in a sales conversation.

You're simply 2 humans discussing a problem the other person is having and whether it's something you can solve for them. If you can, then you should do business together. And the money exchanged is simply a biproduct of that solution.

Happy "selling!"

About the Author
Aleasha Bahr

Meet Aleasha Bahr, a sales strategist, speaker, and the genius behind the Matchmaker Sales Method. With over 14 years of experience, Aleasha excels at tailoring sales strategies to your unique personality, target audience, and service. Her mantra? If it's a fit, it's a fact and there's no selling required.

Aleasha's transformative methods empower business owners to effortlessly convert 80% of their leads, all without resorting to pressure, pitching, or pretending to be someone else. By embracing authenticity and connection, she guides clients towards building genuine relationships with their prospects.

Having achieved outstanding success in her own sales journey, Aleasha boasts a remarkable $50 million+ in services sold. Equally impressive is her track record of helping others generate $15.2 million in sales within the past 3 years alone. Her personalized approach is a proven recipe for success.

Because sales is not a one-size-fits-all!

Your Mission Possible: If you're concerned you need to be sleazy or uncomfortable to successfully sell - this chapter is for you. I break down the never-before -explained process used by people who are "natural" at sales. So, you can easily follow and replicate to make sales in your business while feeling aligned and in integrity.

Get these 5 "honey pot" email follow-up templates now: https://sales.aleashabahr.com/honeypotemail

aleasha@aleashabahr.com
www.aleashabahr.com

Christina Nicholson

Dedication

To my husband Colin. Thank you for doing everything you do for our family.

Chapter 10
Mission Possible:
Become a Media Maven

When I was a TV reporter and anchor, publicists annoyed the hell out of me. They were pushy, self-serving, and didn't help me do my job.

Instead, they were so focused on their own client that I was pushed away, uninterested, and irritated.

The media pitches most publicists sent to the newsrooms I worked in were so cringeworthy that it was apparent they had no idea what journalists, producers, and editors did daily to put together a winning newscast.

FROM TV TO PR

I never believed I would become a freelance publicist and then own a public relations agency with a team of publicists, but here we are.

My journey from TV journalist to publicist to PR agency owner was quick. It happened in just six months.

Having kids, I needed a more flexible schedule than TV news could offer, so I took a big pay cut to work at a local agency where I was promised the opportunity to work from home. Not only was that an empty promise to get me in the door, but my new boss was the king of all micro managers and clock watchers, so I was forced to quit.

In 2016, lots of marketing and PR agencies weren't too comfortable letting their employees work remotely, so I decided to call myself a "professional freelancer" just to be able to work from home.

When I started Media Maven, I had the services part of my business down pat. I knew how to land clients press opportunities without spending money on ads... but that's all I knew.

Add this lack of running a business knowledge to my fear of investing money in Media Maven and you get two years of working 24/7 with inconsistent income and a lot of stress.

It wasn't until I invested in my first business coach that I learned things like how to:

- lead a sales call with a potential client,

- what to pay myself and my growing team,

- and how to sell from stage.

Then, it was time to practice what I preach.

I needed leads, so I began treating myself as a client. That means I started pitching myself to earn media exposure with the goal of wowing small business owners with my expertise so that they'd be itching to work with me by hiring my agency.

But then, other solopreneurs and freelancers would slide into my DMs saying they wanted my help but didn't have a budget to hire an agency. That prompted me to create an online course and community called the Media Mentoring Program.

By using earned media like podcast interviews and online contributing roles, I was able to

- build my email list,

- attract more leads through my website,

- increase my social media following,

- book speaking gigs,

- and close deals faster than ever.

PITCH TO GET PUBLICITY

In 2022, I launched a boot camp called Pitch Publicity Profit. In just three hours, I walk boot campers through how one of my Media Mentoring clients pitched a local TV station, was booked to appear live, and started making brand deals.

This all happened to her in the course of one week. You can make it happen for yourself too by following these steps.

1. Come up with a newsworthy idea.

The biggest mistake people make when they hit send on an email with the goal of earning free attention is making the pitch all about themselves. It reads as if they're asking for a free commercial.

This is not news. It's a promotion, and if you're asking for it, your email might as well be forwarded to the sales team in the offices upstairs.

Instead, you need to ask yourself, "Why should this story be done right now?" That's what Crystal, one of my Media Mentoring Program clients, and I worked on together.

She's a dietitian and was looking for ways to reach more moms in her hometown of San Diego. Her target audience was moms because she had a passion for working with kids.

We started brainstorming a story idea in the fall and decided to capitalize on the couple of weeks when back-to-school news was dominating the headlines. Our pitch addressed the common issue of sending kids to school with a lunch they actually wanted to eat.

After I approved the pitch, Crystal fired it off to a producer for the morning show at a local San Diego TV station.

2. Draft an email that's short, sweet, and to the point.

There were a few things that made this pitch work. The first being that it was not a press release. Press releases aren't only antiquated, but they tend to be long, boring, and overly promotional.

The quickest way to cut through the noise of a busy inbox is to send an email that cuts straight to the chase. In the first sentence, we answered these three questions:

1. Why is this newsworthy now?
2. Who is this for?
3. What is the benefit?

Then we mentioned Crystal's talking points to give the producer an idea of what the segment would look like. When you suggest talking points, it's important to be specific as possible so you're not sharing anything too generic or information we've all heard before.

We followed that up with some hard news, data, and statistics. In this situation, we made the case that this story should be covered not only because it was timely, but also because of the statistics about picky eating and anxiety recently released by the American Academy of Pediatrics.

Finally, we closed the email pitch by sharing why Crystal was the perfect person to talk to about this topic. Not only was she a mom, but she was also a local dietician and nutritionist.

Less than one day later, Crystal was booked to appear that same week. It was her first TV appearance... and she killed it!

To see the exact pitch Crystal sent, word for word, visit ExactPitch.com.

3. Give the media exactly what they want.

Today, members of the media are overworked and underpaid. For that reason, the easier you can make it for them to do their job, the more likely you are to get coverage.

When Crystal showed up for her segment in the wee hours of the morning, she brought lots of healthy snacks, lunch boxes, and pre-arranged meals.

Involvement like this thrills producers. It makes the segment so much better because the visuals are fabulous for morning TV. For that reason, Crystal became a regular on this station and others in the San Diego market.

Regarding other media forms, you may need a great microphone for a podcast interview or high-resolution images for a magazine, for example.

Journalists work on deadlines and if you're not prepared to offer a soundbite or pass along an affiliate link for your book when asked, you will be passed over for someone who is more accessible.

TURN PUBLICITY INTO PROFIT

You may think that after you earn publicity, you sit back and revel in the glory. Lots of people do this... and when they do, they leave money on the table.

The biggest mistake small business owners make after they earn publicity is to assume everyone saw it, heard it, read it, etc., so they don't leverage it.

Here are five things to do after you earn media exposure to turn the publicity into profit.

1. Share it on social media *repeatedly*.

There are so many reasons you should do this.

One is that it's common courtesy to share the coverage someone spent their time and energy to give you. Think of it as a thank you note and recognition to the person who put you on their platform.

The other reason is to show your network you're being featured in the press. It's the best way to let people who already follow you know that you are an expert in your space. It solidifies your reputation with them while building upon it.

2. Tag the journalist, podcast host, media outlet, etc.

A reporter likely won't know you shared your interview on social media if you don't tag them. Now, imagine them actually receiving the thank you note. That's what a tag does. Them noticing this is important because it increases the chance of them coming back to you for future coverage.

I have had clients lose future media opportunities for not sharing their media hits on social media. In today's world where clicks are counted and engagement rates are analyzed, trust me, your post and tag will be noticed and appreciated.

3. Add it to the press page on your website.

Back in the day when you needed to earn a blue checkmark on social media instead of paying for one, a page like this really came in handy.

Today, I like to think of a press page as an archive of all your bragging rights for any visitor to see. It can really set you apart from your competition and wow new website visitors.

4. Include in marketing materials to impress clients, book speaking gigs, sign a book deal, etc.

Assume that no one knows you've earned press coverage before. That's exactly why you need to share it when you market yourself or build your personal brand.

People do business with people they know, like, and trust so including headlines, images, and links of other media outlets singing your praises is the best way to establish your newfound authority.

5. Turn it into a social media advertisement to amplify your credibility and authority.

There is no credibility in advertising, but there is in public relations. So, you can amplify that earned media by putting some ad spend behind it.

This way you're getting the best of both worlds by controlling the message and targeting in the ad while still amplifying that third-party endorsement.

About the Author
Christina Nicholson

Christina Nicholson is a mother of three, TV host, and business owner who lives in Wellington, Florida.

Your Mission Possible: you can get started earning publicity with Christina's free media masterclass 5 Simple Steps to

Getting Featured in the Media Without Spending a Dime at EarnMediaNow.com.

You can also listen to Christina as the host of the Become A Media Maven podcast and get insider tips on building a business without ads at MediaMavenAndMore.com/newsletter

christina@mediamavenandmore.com
www.mediamavenandmore.com

Kiva Slade

Dedication

---

*Thanks to my family for always believing
in me and encouraging me to continue
learning and growing.*

Chapter 11
Mission Possible:
Unleashing the Power of Data

Empowering Women Entrepreneurs
for Sustainable Growth

Picture it, the year is 1996, and President Bill Clinton and Congress have passed the Personal Responsibility and Work Opportunity Act, otherwise known as Welfare Reform. Amid the celebrations, many local, state, and non-profit organizations were trying to figure out the impact on them and those they served. I was in graduate school pursuing my Master's in Public Administration and had an internship at the Baltimore City Housing Authority. The city and the housing authority knew the impact would be dire. Most of the population impacted by this legislation was unskilled and poorly educated. Yet, the mission was to move them from public assistance to work.

While the federal legislation was based on large quantities of data, one of my tasks was to look at the data we knew on the ground specific to those we served. Not only to look at it but translate it to others in the housing authority so it could be actionable.

After grad school, I worked in the hallowed halls that approved that legislation. Data was everywhere. Whether determining the local impact of an appropriations bill or collecting life milestones to demonstrate why someone should have a post office named after them. A common thread continued, breaking the data down so it was actionable. Everyone wanted to know the impact, whether that audience was housing authority officials or voting constituents.

Data surrounds us.

As a business owner, you may feel overwhelmed and frustrated with so many data points. Why? They don't move the needle of your business.

Let's pause momentarily and ensure we are all on the same page. What is data? Merriam-Webster defines data as factual information (such as measurements or statistics) used as a basis for reasoning, discussion, or calculation.

Ok, now let's break it down further.

Factual information, such as measurements or statistics, means numbers. Yes, we could make a case for words, but numbers allow us to measure and compare apples to apples and not oranges. For example, on a scale of 1-5, telling me how much you like tacos will give us more information than an open-ended question on your taco thoughts. A scale of 1-5 gives us a measurement of your feelings about tacos. If I asked every reader their taco rating, I could take that data and make a case for or against tacos. Critically important here is that the claim would be grounded in facts, not feelings. While our feelings play a role in business, we should always look to back them up with data. Facts and feelings should both sit at your data-informed decision-making table.

Continuing our breakdown, data is used for reasoning, discussion, or calculation.

As a business owner, we always seek to maximize our efforts and investments. However, as a service provider or product-based business, you make many daily decisions that impact your business's trajectory. Decisions like deciding which offerings or products to focus your marketing efforts on, how productive your team is, determining the profitability of different products, and more. Data defines the reasoning, discussion, and calculations that go into these decisions.

When you clearly understand your business's data, you can make informed decisions that drive growth and create a solid foundation for success. By tracking key metrics, such as customer acquisition costs, conversion rates, and customer lifetime value, you can identify areas for improvement and optimize your strategies for maximum impact.

Moreover, data can help you identify market trends, consumer preferences, and competitive insights. By analyzing market data and customer feedback, you can refine your offerings, tailor your marketing messages and stay ahead of the competition.

In addition, data can guide your financial decisions and resource allocation. By tracking and analyzing financial data, such as revenue, expenses, and profit margins, you can make informed decisions about budgeting, pricing, and resource allocation, ensuring the optimal use of your resources.

Developing a data-informed and driven mindset and incorporating data into your decision-making processes is essential to harness data's power effectively. This involves establishing clear data collection methods, using analytics tools to track and analyze data, and regularly reviewing and interpreting the data to gain actionable insights.

As a fellow woman business owner, I know there is no shortage of us. Latest statistics suggest women own 42% of the small businesses in the United States. Despite that number, there are still stark disparities in revenue and capital between our companies and those started by men. Despite our record number of business start-ups, our numbers dwindle year after year because businesses often need to be scalable and sustainable. Additionally, because of the service-oriented nature, the companies don't command the same level of investment. The lack of capital is another growth hindrance unless other funding sources, personal or family, are available to support the business.

While the disparity reasons vary, I'm convinced the leveler is data.

You went into business to create an impact. Don't let the lack of data limit your impact and access to capital and resources. Just like Oprah encouraged Toni Braxton to always sign the checks, I want to encourage you always to know the numbers in your business. Track early and often in your business growth. Why? Because you want to build the habit and muscle of incorporating data into your business. Being data-informed is not a luxury in today's economy but a necessity.

Let me circle back to the story's beginning to bring it full circle because I don't want to leave you hanging. My director asked me to complete an analysis of the legislation and its potential impact. We chose a target sample based on data from the Step-Up program, which informed us that most of the population lacked a high school diploma or a GED, which meant transitioning to employment was a difficult challenge. Possession of one of these is always on a job application. We also knew that additional support was needed from other agencies besides the housing authority for "work" to work.

So, diving deep into our target sample population, we crafted a persona and demonstrated the additional support they would need to comply with the law. This information was used to build a new initiative incorporating sister agencies, social services, education, and health to unite and successfully move people from welfare to work. It was a significant undertaking, but we let the data guide us.

As a woman entrepreneur, you have the power to leverage data to drive your business forward and achieve your goals. So, embrace the data-driven approach, and let the numbers guide you toward success.

About the Author
Kiva Slade

Kiva Slade is the owner and founder of The 516 Collaborative, specializing in providing comprehensive support to small business owners at the intersection of data and operations. With a Master's degree in Public Administration and certifications as a Director of Operations and Online Business Manager, Kiva brings over 20 years of experience in the public and private sectors.

Throughout her career, Kiva has demonstrated a remarkable ability to drive results and achieve success, whether as a Legislative Director for a member of Congress or as the chief encouragement officer for her children.

When not immersed in business endeavors, you can find Kiva savoring gluten-free desserts or engrossed in the pages of a captivating book. Her passion for helping entrepreneurs thrive and her commitment to excellence make her an invaluable asset to any business seeking growth and operational excellence.

Your Mission Possible: Learn to unlock the power of data and achieve sustainable growth. Let's harness the potential of data-driven decisions and redefine the future of women's entrepreneurship.

hello@the516collaborative.com
www.the516collaborative.com

MISSION POSSIBLE

Anna Paszkiet and Jen Hall

Dedication

To our families for supporting us through every triumph and challenge!

Chapter 12
Mission Possible:
Build Your Community

It All Begins and Grows with Community

Now that you've learned all that is possible to become a successful entrepreneur, let's explore how community involvement can bolster your journey to success!

Imagine starting your day with a problem in your business. The people around you work in the corporate world and can't relate. You aren't stressed though because you've found a community of like-minded entrepreneurs to call upon. You're able to jump online, post your problem, and ask for help. By the end of the day, you've received dozens of tips and offers to help solve your dilemma. Some people are even offering to jump on a call with you to strategically talk everything through. This is the power of having a strong community and why we believe you should either start one of your own or find one that fits your personality.

Stacey M had been making great strides with her confidence-building guided journals and workshops for kids. She felt she had been able to reach her target audience but sensed a plateau in her growth and craved fresh perspectives and innovative ideas. That's when she joined the Ambition to Success Community. The women in the community come from different backgrounds, have unique businesses, and are at various stages of their entrepreneurial journeys.

The community dissected how we talk about our businesses. In the past, Stacey talked about her mission as helping kids feel more confident and understand that they are worthy. Based on the group discussion and feedback, she shifted her focus to her experiences as a mom, and she was able to identify her ideal customer as other moms. She started talking about her business using a mom-to-mom approach. Putting this new approach to the test at an event, Stacey immediately noticed a significant difference in her ability to engage customers. By speaking directly to other moms, sharing her personal journey, and understanding their unique needs, she forged a deeper connection.

Thanks to the support and feedback she found in the community, Stacey is breaking free from stagnation. She is excited to see where this journey will take her, and she's grateful for the incredible support network she's found along the way.

We are Anna Paszkiet and Jen Hall, the founders of a group coaching program called Ambition to Success. We provide women entrepreneurs with an accessible and supportive community to help grow their business. Included in the program is a monthly entrepreneur experience box that includes items and services that support business and personal development growth. Each box supports small businesses, and we believe that finding yourself an amazing community is the key to business success.

> 66
>
> *"If you want to go quickly, go alone. If you want to go far, go together."*
> *– African Proverb*

Being an entrepreneur can be lonely if you don't have a community of like-minded people to support you, challenge you and lift you up. Finding the right community can give you the tools you need to face the day-to-day challenges of owning and running your own business. But not just any group will do. You need to find the right community of people that will benefit you both personally and professionally.

5 BENEFITS TO BEING PART OF A COMMUNITY

1. Mastermind - Being a part of a community is like having your own mastermind group-as long as you are an active member. Being part of a solid mastermind allows multiple perspectives. You can ask for help with problems, get opinions on new ideas, and ask for support with your online social channels, among so many other things... The wonderful thing about a mastermind is you also give that support back to other group members. Your opinion and thoughts matter just as equally as the next. It's a solid place to help you grow your business.

The Ambition to Success community lets us know regularly that they are connecting with people outside of the community and brainstorming ideas for each other's businesses. There is no greater compliment than to hear about people connecting and helping each other because they connected through your community.

2. Referrals - A tight knit and active community allows you to build your brand's know, like, and trust factor (KLT Factor). The KLT Factor is essential if you want to build a successful brand and business. Being part of a community allows you to form authentic relationships with other members and fosters mutual trust. This trust is what results in referrals. When you get to know someone and trust what they do, you want to refer them, and they will want to refer you. We all need to get outside of our circles of people we know to grow our businesses. Referrals outside of our own audience are a win-win for all!

3. Accountability - When we set goals, we are accountable for taking ownership of our own actions. Sometimes that's really hard to do and we benefit from being accountable to someone else. Business owners who understand how a business operates and what you go through on a daily basis can make amazing accountability partners. When working towards big goals, it's important to be around those who can lift you up and cheer you on but also let you vent when you need to instead of giving up.

We had someone in our group who was terrified to go live on Facebook and with some cheering on from the group she was able to go live, get amazing feedback from the community and continues to go live regularly.

4. Education - You are an expert in your field. Being a part of a community allows you to share your knowledge with the group and learn from other people at the same time. We can't know everything, and this allows you to move forward with your big goals and your day-to-day operations. A community allows us to learn from those who have come before us and may offer us a different way of looking at things.

We have someone who is a part of our community who came in thinking something very specific because of her background. After having a lively discussion with the community her energy shifted, she had some new ideas and was able to put them in motion to have a successful week.

As we like to say...

You don't know what you don't know, so getting someone else's knowledge on a topic can be crucial for moving your business forward.

5. Mindset - Entrepreneurs have a different mindset than those in the corporate world. Being an entrepreneur means that you always have to be ready to pivot. It means staying positive even when things are not going your way. You want to be surrounded by people who understand what is happening and have a growth vs fixed mindset.

Adopting a growth mindset is a necessary skill for entrepreneurs to master but one that is not easy. Being in a community that encourages you to overcome challenges and view them as opportunities is better than one who focuses on setbacks and views them as failures.

Sue J is an amazing artist in our community. She however didn't see herself as an artist and NEVER called herself one. One day we asked her to say, "I am an artist." She paused after delivering that statement and everyone on the call cheered her on. She said again, "I am an artist!," and it took a minute to compose herself afterwards. While everyone else saw her as an artist she did not see herself as one. She showed up differently after that call and owned that she indeed was an artist.

Choosing the right community requires some diligence and maybe even some trial and error. Not every group you come across is going to be the right fit for you and your business. How do you decide what is right for you?

Make sure you are not the smartest person in the group. The group you choose should challenge you to be better. The group you choose should leave room for you to grow. The group you choose should be one you feel great going into each day. It should be one that you participate in both helping others and asking questions for yourself. It's ok to try many groups before you find one that works best for you.

Consider creating your own community. The group you create should bring together like-minded people surrounding a core topic (business owners, stay at home moms, authors, etc.). Creating a strong thriving community takes consistency, a welcoming attitude, knowing your audience, and a basic knowledge of analytics.

There are many tools designed to help entrepreneurs grow their business. Finding the right community is the final step and a key for growth, learning new skills, and taking your ambition and turning it into success!

About the Authors
Anna Paszkiet and Jen Hall

Anna Paszkiet is a Digital Marketing Strategist with over 20 years in the Marketing Industry. She worked in the corporate world first with a media marketing company for 10 years then with smaller companies to expand their marketing and reach the communities they were located in. In 2018 she left to start her own marketing business helping other businesses. While she loved doing this, she wasn't helping as many businesses as she would like and ended up co-founding Ambition to Success. Her focus is on business growth and marketing so your business can create an online presence and grow profitably.

Jen Hall is a Veteran of the United States Air Force where she served her country as an Air Traffic Controller. She is a Certified Aromatherapist who built a successful business and community online following the diagnosis of a degenerative spinal disease. In 2015, Jen used her experience to become a Social Media Manager and Social Media Marketing Strategist. She has helped small business owners and large organizations turn six-figure profits, expand their marketing reach, meet sales goals, acquire new leads, and retain long-term customers and clients. Jen is the co-founder of Ambition to Success. Her focus is on building a community so that women entrepreneurs feel empowered and supported on their journey to achieving success.

Your Mission Possible: Being an entrepreneur can be lonely if you don't have a community of like-minded people to support you, challenge you and lift you up. Finding the right community can give you the tools you need to face the day-to-day challenges of owning and running your own business. But not just any group will do. We'll share with you how to find the right community that will benefit you both personally and professionally.

letstalk@ambitiontosuccess.com
www.ambitiontosuccess.com

Conclusion

Mission Possible #6 Money Mindset

MINDSET LESSON: You don't have to know everything and do everything the right way right out of the gate. It sounds cliché, but it's true - business ownership, like everything else in life, is a journey. You learn, grow, and change over time. It's taken Stacy over 15 years of business and over 50 years of living to get to this point, and there is still so much to learn!

Mission Possible #7 Brand + Website Design

Establishing a brand that aligns with your values and speaks to your target audience is crucial for success. Jenny guides you through the key elements of branding, including defining your brand personality, mission statement, and target audience. We'll also delve into the importance of having a website and how it can enhance your brand's credibility and online presence. You'll learn how to create a website that's not only visually captivating but strategically designed to attract your ideal client. By the end of this chapter, you'll have a solid grasp of the building blocks required to develop a strong brand and website for your business. With the right tools and strategies, you can build a thriving brand that resonates with your audience. So, let's dive in and have some fun!

Mission Possible #8 Launch your offer confidently

Remember that in business, almost everything is "normal." Six-figure launch followed by a five-figure launch? Normal. Facebook ads work one launch and not so well the next? Normal. Deliver the most beautiful open cart transition one launch and stumble over your words the next one? Normal. Tech gremlins at play out of the blue? Normal. Feeling high off of the launch experience one time, then dread it the next? Normal.

People post highlights only on IG, so remember that as you launch your new program or course. It takes time. Hallie reminds us that each launch will build on the next. You are never "done," but you will see consistent success when you follow the process and take imperfect action.

Mission Possible #9 Selling like a natural

Being a natural takes practice. When someone is a fit, you're going to tell them why. It makes it very easy to transition to the sale and "asking for the business" because if it's a fit, it's a fact, and there's no selling involved. Aleasha reminds us that you're not a gross person taking someone's money. You're a mother, sister, daughter, friend - just like the human sitting across from you in a sales conversation. You're simply two humans discussing a problem the other person is having and whether it's something you can solve for them. If you can, then you should do business together. And the money exchanged is simply a by-product of that solution. Happy "selling"!

Mission Possible #10 Become a Media Maven

When I was a TV reporter and anchor, publicists annoyed the hell out of me. They were pushy, self-serving, and didn't help me do my job. Instead, they were so focused on their own client that

I was pushed away, uninterested, and irritated. The media pitches most publicists sent to the newsrooms I worked in were so cringeworthy that it was apparent they had no idea what journalists, producers, and editors did daily to put together a winning newscast.

Christina says the quickest way to cut through the noise of a busy inbox is to send an email that cuts straight to the chase. In the first sentence, we answered these three questions:

1. Why is this newsworthy now?
2. Who is this for?
3. What is the benefit?

Mission Possible #11 Unleashing the Power of Data

When you clearly understand your business's data, you can make informed decisions that drive growth and create a solid foundation for success. By tracking key metrics, such as customer acquisition costs, conversion rates, and customer lifetime value, you can identify areas for improvement and optimize your strategies for maximum impact. Moreover, data can help you identify market trends, consumer preferences, and competitive insights. By analyzing market data and customer feedback, you can refine your offerings, tailor your marketing messages, and stay ahead of the competition, according to Kiva.

Developing a data-informed and driven mindset and incorporating data into your decision-making processes is essential to harness data's power effectively. This involves establishing clear data collection methods, using analytics tools to track and analyze data, and regularly reviewing and interpreting the data to gain actionable insights.

Mission Possible #12 Build Your Own Community

Consider creating your own community. The group you create should bring together like-minded people surrounding a core topic (business owners, stay-at-home moms, authors, etc.). Building a strong, thriving community takes consistency, a welcoming attitude, knowing your audience, and basic analytics knowledge. There are many tools designed to help entrepreneurs grow their business. As Anna and Jen tell us, finding the right community is the final step and a key for growth, learning new skills, and turning your ambition into success!

Your Mission Possible: Next Steps

Melanie Herschorn

No matter what your Mission Possible is, you have the inner strength to achieve it.

And now, you have the manual for success in entrepreneurship. Be sure to refer back often, whenever you need a boost of motivation and guidance.

Mission Possible for women entrepreneurs is about embracing a success mindset and garnering skills to take on what others think is impossible. It is also so much more.

Welcome to the Mission Possible movement, where we believe that humans are not meant to be confined within the limitations that others impose on us. When we dare to dream big and set audacious goals that stretch the boundaries of what is deemed possible, we unlock our true potential to not only transform our own lives but also leave an indelible impact on the world as a whole.

One of our primary goals is to provide a constant source of inspiration and unwavering support across diverse industries and disciplines. We strive to amplify the voices of individuals who have compelling stories to share, ensuring that their narratives reach wider audiences. We are dedicated to creating an inclusive space where ideas can flourish, and personal growth is fostered.

Opportunities for you to join the Mission Possible movement will range from thought-provoking books to immersive workshops and retreats. We value the pursuit of knowledge, recognizing that it is through continuous learning and the guidance of experienced mentors that we can achieve greatness. We aim to foster a strong sense of community, understanding that when surrounded by like-minded individuals who share in your vision, the possibilities become boundless.

Let's break free from the confines of conventional thinking and embark on a mission to accomplish the seemingly impossible. Together, we will create a world where aspirations are nurtured, dreams are realized, and every individual is empowered to defy boundaries and shape their own destiny.

With the right mindset, unwavering determination, and the support of a vibrant community, nothing can stand in the way of our collective potential.

That is Mission Possible. For more details and to get special gifts from each of the authors, visit www.MissionPossibleSeries.com.

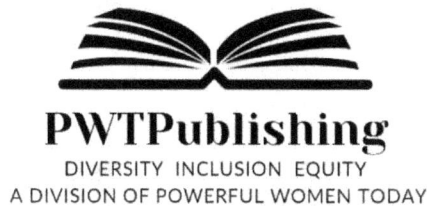

MISSION POSSIBLE

PWTPublishing
DIVERSITY INCLUSION EQUITY
A DIVISION OF POWERFUL WOMEN TODAY